An Outstretched Hand

by

Dr. Wright L. Lassiter, Jr.
Wright L. Lassiter, III

Order this book online at www.trafford.com
or email orders@trafford.com

Most Trafford titles are also available at major online book retailers.

Co-authored by Wright L. Lassiter, III
Cover Design by Eddie Walker

Note for Librarians: A cataloguing record for this book is available from Library
and Archives Canada at www.collectionscanada.ca/amicus/index-e.html

Printed in Victoria, BC, Canada.

ISBN: 978-1-4251-8824-5

*We at Trafford believe that it is the responsibility of us all, as both individuals
and corporations, to make choices that are environmentally and socially sound.
You, in turn, are supporting this responsible conduct each time you purchase a
Trafford book, or make use of our publishing services. To find out how you are
helping, please visit www.trafford.com/responsiblepublishing.html*

*Our mission is to efficiently provide the world's finest, most comprehensive
book publishing service, enabling every author to experience success.
To find out how to publish your book, your way, and have it available
worldwide, visit us online at www.trafford.com*

www.trafford.com

North America & international
toll-free: 1 888 232 4444 (USA & Canada)
phone: 250 383 6864 ♦ fax: 250 383 6804
email: info@trafford.com

The United Kingdom & Europe
phone: +44 (0)1865 487 395 ♦ local rate: 0845 230 9601
facsimile: +44 (0)1865 481 507 ♦ email: info.uk@trafford.com

10 9 8 7 6 5 4 3 2 1

TABLE OF CONTENTS

PART III
PARENTS AND THEIR CHILDREN

PART IV
GUIDANCE FOR LIFE'S JOURNEY

PART V
END NOTES

DEDICATION

TO

Bessie Ryan Lassiter
Wife, Life Partner, Mother, Grandmother

Cathy Race Lassiter
Wife, Mother, Helpmate

Michele Lassiter-Ewell
First Child & Sister
Mother, Helpmate

Cylton Ewell
Brother-in-law
Son-in-law
Father

Ryan Simone Ewell
First grandchild

Loren Jenae Lassiter
Second grandchild

AN OUTSTRETCHED HAND

Each of us was made by God
And some of us grew tall.
Others stood out in the wind
Their branches bent and fell.
Those of us who walk in light
Must help the ones in darkness up

For that's what life is all about
And love is all there is to life.

Each of us was made by God,
Beautiful in His mind's eye.
Those of us that turned out sound
Should look across our shoulders once
And help the weak ones to their feet.

It only takes an outstretched hand!

PREFACE

LIFE CAN BE BEAUTIFUL

When I look out the glass walls from my family room, across the pool, I see the large rear yard, and I can actually hear the grass growing. I can marvel over the splendor of the large shady trees. I think, "Everything is so lush and green. There's beauty all around me."

Life can be very beautiful, even in the darkest of times, if we choose to see it so. I am deeply impressed with what renowned author, Chuck Swindoll states, "your attitude determines your altitude." This is most certainly true as we seek to be the best fathers we can be. Years ago when my two adult children were growing up, I found that when I caught and cherished those little things they did, I was better equipped to keep my attitude at a higher altitude. The same is true now when I am around my two, rapidly growing, grand daughters.

These little things have huge impact if I choose to let them into my heart. It's one of the grand daughter's attempts to teach me the message associated with her favorite cartoon show. Or when the other one teaches me the latest fashions. It's learning to laugh when they both critique the way I prepare their lunches when their grandmother is away, or when their parents are not around. "They don't fix it that way." It's the sound of their uncontrollable giggling in my library when they are engrossed in their game boys.

Catching hold of these huge little things can be quite challenging, however. They are fleeting and elusive, especially when we're feeling the weight of the world on our shoulders. Work-related pressures, strained relationships and fatigue can interfere with our ability to pick them up on our radar screen.

But as fathers, we need to be diligent in keeping the radar screen clear and letting those once-in-a-lifetime moments with our little ones sink deep into our souls. When we allow that to happen these results can emerge in our lives:

- We build our children and grand children's self image.
- We communicate love to our children.
- We become more nurturing as fathers and grandfathers.
- We teach our children what's really important.
- We build a bank of memories that can keep us close with our children (and grand children) during difficult times.
- We foster closeness with the parents of our children, or with your child's mother.

So, my advice is, keep your periscope up and hold on to those huge little things for all they're worth.

This is the inspiration that caused me and my son to assemble thoughts and ideas that could benefit other fathers, prospective fathers, and family members in general.

Dr. Wright L. Lassiter, Jr.

FOREWORD

Before the time of Abraham, the notion of fatherhood has been a stalwart of societies. The first book of the Bible extols the complexities of the earliest virtues of fatherhood in the relationship of the maker to His creation in Adam. This scenario depicts perhaps the initial tug of parent to child dynamics and the earliest references to parental obedience (dis.)

J. Hampton Keathley, in an article cited in Bible.org states that the Deuteronomy verses are not just a passage with principles for the home, but "it is a call to obedience for God's glory, as an evidence of love for God and for a ministry to the world through the perpetuation of faith in the Lord from <u>generation to generation</u>. Note the principles in Deuteronomy 6:1-2: "Now this is the commandment, the statutes and the judgments which the Lord, your God, has commended me to teach you, that you might do them in the land where you are going over to possess it. So that you and your son and your grandson might fear the Lord your God, to keep all His statutes and His commandments, which I command you, all the days of your life, and that you days may be prolonged.

This illustration of the omnipotent father is again restated in Deuteronomy 4:10-11. "Remember the day you stood before the Lord your God at Horeb, when the Lord said to me, 'Assemble the people to Me, that I may let them hear My words so they may learn to fear Me all the days they live on the earth, and that they may teach their children.' "And you came near and stood at the foot of the mountain, and the mountain burned with fire in the very heart of the heavens; darkness, cloud and thick gloom." While we would not want to approximate Wright Lassiter's experience in this realm to God, we certainly want to under gird the fundamental belief in this greatest of powers.

References to a patriarchal society are rampant in both lay and biblical accounts. The fundamental basis of these references are squarely grounded in the premise of God's relationship to His creation, His children, His heirs. The belief or perspective that God represents a masculine gender has been long debated. Critics argue that the authors of the bible inspired or not, were men and largely represent a pervasive, if not bias assumption relative to God's gender. We might argue that if one truly believes, it matters little or not whether God is masculine, feminine or even defies man's comprehension of gender.

Certainly there are examples in nature of dual sex organism that challenge conventional wisdom. The identification of the holy trinity which embodies father, son and Holy Spirit has generated significant debate over the gender composition of the Holy Spirit. This debate leads us to an important point in this discussion of fatherhood in the present context. What role does, should father's play in the contemporary Christian family? And more specifically, what role should African American Christian fathers play in the family.

An unlikely source of data from the Center for Marriage and Families and specifically the Child Wellbeing study suggest that the church attendance of fathers, in urban communities, is a powerful predictor of relationship quality and marital behavior. Some 95% of men in urban communities who attend church are significantly more likely to father children only after marriage. The frequently asked, perhaps rhetorical question is so beyond the biological necessity for fathers, what do they bring to the equation. Historically, it was thought and largely practiced that fathers brought discipline as the authority figure. That they helped children prepare for the often harsh realities of the outside world and that they were the primary breadwinners and providers. The Biblical reference in Genesis 48:15 frequently and sometimes metaphorically describes the father as shepherd to a flock. We also find the literature replete with references to fathers as the leader, protector and wise counselor. Titus 2:6 states that the older men (fathers) should be taught "to be temperate, worthy of respect, self-controlled, sound in faith in love and in endurance."

The present reality of the African American family frequently, but certainly not exclusively, offers a stark contrast to those traditional roles of harsh disciplinarian, where the simple invocation of "wait until your dad gets home" was enough to straighten the most discordant behavior. Juxtapose this tradition to a situation where there is often no male presence and sometimes a non-custodial, non-related adult male with no ties and/or responsibility for the children of a household. More than likely, the adult male himself has little or no experience, or tutelage from another male parental figure. The juvenile male in this circumstance may receive no guidance on how to be a responsible, caring, but yet strong personality and may frequently mirror what he sees both at home and in the community.

Add to this scenario that the chances are that this adult male is unemployed or under-employed and has little or no college or technical professional education. It is a formula for disaster. I am told that private, prison systems project the number of beds needed to house inmates on the failure and dropout rate of 4th graders, and particularly in urban school districts. The author posits that "if children are encouraged by their parents (fathers) to develop a sense of responsibility, they will gain the assurance they need. And when children gain a high sense of self worth, their chances of attaining their life goals is greatly increased." Here we are led to believe that the nurturing role of fathers and mothers is critical to healthy child development.

We must ponder the delicate balance of thoughts and actions that must have flowed through Wright Lassiter, Jr.'s mind as he wrestled with the vagaries of the Jim Crow south and whatever comfort was extended by the protective envelope of parents, friends, mentors and the intellectual bastion called Tuskegee University. Had there not have been a strong fatherly presence in Wright Lassiter's life, might he have fallen prey to the vestiges of self-doubt and lack of persistence, a certain formula for failure even today.

Had it not been for a strong fatherly presence would he have faltered in his pursuit of those inalienable rights of freedom, liberty and the pursuit of happiness we hold near and dear. Basic human rights denied to some simply because of race and ethnicity and not based on any principle of meritocracy or performance. A simple set of limiting circumstances, in a point of time, which were reinforced by practice and sometimes law. His grasp of the magnitude of this set of circumstances heightened the need to understand the significance of knowledge and education, and he made certain that he, his children and as many as he could influence would not be ravaged by the cancer of ignorance. Anyone with experience or even knowledge of Mississippi and Alabama in the 1940, 50s, 60s, and even the 70s, knows well the challenges to African Americans' personhood, fatherhood, and yes, even manhood during those periods. How might have these confluent elements shaped the man, the father, the granddad? Clearly, God provided Wright Lassiter, Jr. with guidance and inspiration to overcome life's hurdles, and to advise and counsel his children and a legacy of young men and women who have benefited from the lessons of his journey. A journey, by the way that is far from over.

As the sojourn continues, it gives us an opportunity to fast forward a bit to the now and the near term future. And it finds us in the midst of a massive effort to address one of the most critical, though not necessarily acknowledged challenges of our time—the plight of African American men. The primary audience for this effort is young men 15-30 years old who are documentably, an endangered species.

This group represents better than 50% of high school and college dropouts, 60% of the U.S. prison population (18% of the U.S. male population), only 4% of college graduates and 90% of the chronically unemployed. What has this to do with a book on fatherhood, or Wright Lassiter, Jr. and his son Wright Lassiter, III for that matter, I would argue everything. If the lessons followed and practiced by the author give us anything, it perhaps provides us with a roadmap and a simple set of guiding principles for the lives of fathers, young and mature.

As a member of the President's Roundtable, an organization of African American presidents, chancellors and leaders in the community college sector, Wright Lassiter again has an opportunity to help shape the legacy of fathers and fathers-to-be. The President's Roundtable hosted a national summit on April 6, 2008 with representation from two- and four-year colleges and universities, civic and fraternal organizations, civil rights entities, foundations and a myriad of non-profit and community-based organizations. The goal was to coalesce the disparate and largely singular efforts of these organizations around the issue of lack of attendance and persistence of African American males in high school and college.

Utilizing the considerable resources, both human and capital of these organizations, a national steering team is being formed, short-term and long-range strategies are being developed and policy and implications are being formulated. Proverbs 14:4 asserts that "Where there are no oxen, the manger is empty, but from the strength of the ox comes an abundant harvest." Again, you may ask about the relationship of this effort to this book. I feel privileged to respond in this way. As we improve the attendance and persistence of African American boys and men in high school and college we also exponentially improve the odds that these young men will become productive citizens and fathers. A more well-educated adult male populations should be less involved with the criminal justice system, reduce the number of adults incarcerated in jail and prison, and lower overall crime rates.

A by-factor is an attendant increase in civic engagement, increased voting rates and volunteerism, and a strengthening of political democracy. Better educated male adults, especially past age 30, are more likely to be married and living with their spouses and children. They are also less likely to father children out of wedlock, more likely to help increase marriage rates, strengthen family life, reduce family poverty and dependency, and improve the future economic prospects of the nation's children. Increasing the future number of adult men with postsecondary degrees and certificates should help lower aggregate unemployment and reduce structural unemployment problems in the nation's labor markets. The author asserts that young black men are being destroyed in record numbers in this country. The question is—what can be done by men, fathers, you and me, both short term and long term, to stem the tide.

The Lassiter father and son duo believe that there are no quick fixes to this problem, as there are to the challenges and rewards of fatherhood. The senior author also believes that just as nuclear and extended family was instrumental in his life and the life of his son, the same intensity of efforts is needed today. Proverbs 13:22 suggest that "A good man leaves an inheritance for his children's children, but a sinner's wealth is stored up for the righteous." The author's hope is that the printed words of wisdom and caution on these pages will suffice to begin to engage all of us in a life-long journey of commitment. Proverbs 14:8 is a fitting conclusion to the words contained in this foreword: "The wisdom of the prudent is to give thought to their ways, but the folly of fools is deception."

Andrew C. Jones, Ed.D.
Vice Chancellor for Educational Affairs
Dallas County Community College District

PART I

BACKGROUND AND SETTING

THE CHALLENGE IN PERSPECTIVE
THE FATHER'S VIEW

As an educator, ordained minister and community servant, I have dedicated my life to "stretching out my hand" to assist, lift up and encourage persons. This calling in my life came as a result of strong family ties; compassionate, concerned and competent teachers; extended families who were always "watching out" for young boys and girls; and the powerful influence of the neighborhood church and its pastor. At every turn those influential people and forces in my life planted and nurtured seeds that extolled the benefits of education, and how education was the imperative for freedom, liberation, and a productive life.

The words of my father at an early age became a core value that was burned into my consciousness—"If you want to get ahead, get something in your head."

Although my parents had not attended college during my education years, college was established as something that was within reach. That is, if I had the fortitude, will, and the "holy common sense" to get it done. I was the first of my nine brothers and sisters to attend college. I came away from that experience not only equipped for a yet-to-be-developed professional life, but I learned the essence of what is now known as "servant leadership."

My father also imparted another key lesson that became a key core value: "Service is the rent that you pay for the space that you occupy on the earth that God created." In later years he added a valuable post script to that mantra when he said: "Junior, always strive to live in a high rent district."

Childhood experiences, the impact of family, friends and teachers, my college experiences, as well as "lessons of life learned along the way," were instrumental in preparing, molding and shaping me for a life of service.

The confluence of all of those elements, along with further preparation, mentoring, and hard work, has enabled me to attain positions rarely attained by others. Many of my achievements in life caused me to be the "first" African American.

As a junior in college in 1954, it fell my lot, purely by accident, to integrate the payroll office of the Spencer Chemical Works. I was privileged to become the first African American chairman of the Tuskegee (Alabama) Housing Authority and had the challenge of integrating that agency following the passage of the Civil Rights Act of 1965. On a trip by car from Baltimore to our home in Tuskegee, my wife and two children joined me when we became the first African American family to walk in the front door and be registered as guests at the Rome (Georgia) Hotel after the passage of the Civil Rights Act of 1964. I became the first African American president of a college in the State University of New York System when I was elected president of Schenectady County Community College. While serving in New York it fell my lot to join with a Jewish friend and the two of us integrated the formerly all-white Mohawk Club in Schenectady, New York. Since moving to Dallas the list of "firsts" has continued, starting with being the first African American to serve as chairman of the board of the United Way of Metropolitan Dallas. Then there was service on corporate and community service boards—again the "first," and a long list of awards—again being the "first."

Each time that I became a "first," my immediate thought was that I must work to ensure that there would be "second's and third's." I have always viewed any achievement as a reflection of the trust and confidence that my family, friends, teachers, and colleagues had in me. With each pinnacle scaled, I humbly took note that I was standing on the shoulders of others.

It is the confluence of a rich array of experiences that caused me and my son to decide to produce a small work that could be used by parents, children and family members as they labor to mold their children.

While my son did not have to experience directly the difficult years that I did, he was a careful observer as he progressed from childhood to the youthful period, and finally as an adult. I am proud to say that he has followed in my footsteps and embraced those core values that were pivotal in shaping my life.

The brief essays in this book combine insights with spiritual truths from the treasure trove that we both embrace—the Bible. In the fast-paced world that we now live in, where change is exponential, where there is an overwhelming focus on immediate gratification, and there is an attitude that "I can do it all by myself," there is something vital missing.

We are not invincible. In spite of our education, and a wealth of advantages, we all have to acknowledge the truth that there is a supreme power. That power is the everlasting God as evidenced through the life, death, resurrection and example of Jesus Christ. There is no limit to the power that God, through Jesus Christ, can have in our lives. Scripture informs us that "I can do all things through Him who strengthens me." How much more successful we would be; how much more fruitful our lives would be; how much stronger and resilient our homes and families would be, if we could take the truth of the Scriptures to heart in all that we do.

A father and his son have spanned the chasm of time to produce a simple work designed to encourage, empower, and to enlist men in the awesome task of shaping and molding their children—with a special focus on the male.

You may ask—why the male? A 2006 report from the Schott Foundation is eye-opening. Ponder these statistics:

- A large number of black young men in the United States don't graduate from high school. Only 35% of the young black male student population graduated from high school in Chicago and only 26% of the young black male student population in New York City graduate from high school. On a national basis, 58% of black boys in this country do not graduate from high school.
- Nationally, only 22% of or young black men finish college.

- Young black male college students have the highest dropout rate and the lowest grades while in school.
- When our young black men are not successful in college, they are much more likely to succeed in the nation's criminal justice system.
- There are more black men in prisons and jails in the United States than there are black men incarcerated in the entire rest of the world (over 1.1 million)
- Black male students as young as six years old are being arrested daily in catastrophic numbers in the United States. In the eyes of many, education is on lock-down.
- According to a Joint Economic Committee Study chaired by Senator Charles Schumer (D-NY), 37.7% of our young black men in this country are not working at all!
- Almost 70% of black children in this country are born into female, single-parent households based on the 2000 Census.
- In Texas blacks comprised 12% of the total population, but made up 44% of the total prison population in 2000.

The lives of our young black men are being destroyed in record numbers in this country. The question is—what we can do, both short term and long term, to save them?

There are no "quick fix" solutions. However, we believe that just as family figures were instrumental in the life of this father and his son, the same is needed today. We are hopeful that the words of wisdom on these printed pages will serve a useful purpose to the readers.

THE CHALLENGE IN PERSPECTIVE
THE SON'S VIEW

In contrast to my father, I grew up in what most would consider a privileged environment. Our family milieu was stable and nurturing. My sister and I were exposed to consistently positive influences and those experiences were instrumental in shaping our core values, and our outlook on life. We lived in a classic example of the middle-class American lifestyle. These circumstances are too frequently considered the exception rather than the rule—particularly in the African American community.

I am the clear and grateful beneficiary of many "Outstretched Hands" during the course of my life. Those hands have taken the form of loving parents, supportive grandparents and other extended family members, a "village" of concerned parents in communities in which I have lived, school teachers, college professors and administrators, athletic coaches and career mentors.

My household as a child was typified by strong parental influence. A father who modeled the best of what fatherhood had to offer: (1) a Christ-centered perspective; (2) a loving family (with my father imparting key lessons that he learned from his father and, in turn, saw them firsthand from him and my grandfather); (3) seeing firsthand the intricacies of what it means to have a demanding, but deeply satisfying career by seeing the example of my father; and (4) sustaining friendships.

My mother served as the consummate matriarch. She was the glue that held the family together. She filled in all the gaps, handled the details, and provided an adequate balance of freedom to allow her children to explore and grow, paired with enlightened micromanagement at times when parental guidance needed to be active and "on-the-ground."

Very early in life, my parents focused my attention on core values that would support a productive and successful adult life. Those standards included hard work, honesty, integrity, compassion, discipline and humility. They preached the importance of an advanced education—college paired with graduate and/or professional degrees—and extolled a childhood life pattern that would create the foundation for the attainment of such. As a child, I heard constant echoes that created a positive self-image and fostered confidence. My sister and I consistently heard these messages: "Always know that you are as good as anyone else you encounter, but never carry yourself as though you are better than others." "If you want to get ahead, get something in your head."

Throughout my formative years, I was further blessed by having the incredible example of leaders who shaped my development outside of the immediate family. Growing up in a small town in the Deep South—Tuskegee, Alabama—I benefited from a "community of parents" who actively shared in shaping the development of the youth in our neighborhood. An early figure with "outstretched hands," was our neighbor, Mr. Thomas Hardwick. I can remember going onto our front porch and would call out to "Hardwick" when he was doing work in his yard, or polishing his car. He would always talk with me. He was a graduate of Tuskegee Institute and had been an outstanding varsity basketball player and later a coach. I picked up key lessons from him.

As an elementary student, at St. Joseph's Catholic School in Tuskegee, I recall the influence of Mr. Thomas, the principal. A sturdy African American man, he modeled values similar to those patterned at home. He exuded a strong personality, and held quite high expectations for his students. He was stern, yet a caring parental eye was evident in his interactions with me and my classmates. So, at a very young age, I was exposed to a responsible authoritarian who modeled success. While I am certain that I was not consciously cognizant of this influence, his example clearly shaped my life at a very early age. I could see the "connection" between what I experienced with my family and the growing "larger world."

There were interesting life moments during our life in the somewhat sheltered community of Tuskegee, Alabama. The college environment became a "way of life." My father's work and other interests exposed me to new experiences in a unique way. I can remember when he and Dean K.B. Young took me along when they visited the ROTC students from the university at their summer camp. Just by observing the cadets I picked up vital leadership lessons. I still remember when my father gave me an opportunity to engage in some of the activities that included weapons practice. I saw an example of risk-taking when he engaged in the airborne training activity of jumping from the 50-foot tower.

My father was an Army Reserve officer and he always found ways to expose me and my sister to that part of his life. I took great delight when he would take the family to the Officer's Club at the nearby Maxwell Field Air Force Base for dinner and other festive occasions. That experience continued when the family would join him at Fort Rucker, Alabama during the two-week summer training period for his military unit. He still reminds me of how I would always order the "largest items" on the menu.

My parents also exposed me to the opportunity to participate in activities where I would be "on my own." Two such incidents stand out. They took me to a week-long activity for boys in Georgia. My mother had reservations about her son being away from the family, but I recall my father saying "he will be o.k." They were both pleased when they had unloaded my trunk and gave me my instructions, put me in the hands of the camp leader, and I said a quick "bye—see you later," and dashed off to be with the others in the camp. When they came back to pick me up, they were told that I had been one of the camp leaders.

There was another time when Mrs. Helen Mahone took a group of middle-school students to Disney World in Orlando. Once again I was "on my own," and I relished the opportunity to function in a somewhat independent fashion. When we returned from that trip Mrs. Mahone told my parents that I had been one of the "junior chaperones."

As our family moved northward to the Atlantic Coast at the conclusion of my seventh grade, I was exposed to a larger community situated just between Washington, D.C. and Baltimore, Maryland. In the planned community of Columbia, Maryland, at Wilde Lake

High School, I encountered a duo of men who perhaps influenced me more than any other individuals outside of my namesakes—my father and grandfather. As a nearly six-foot tall ninth grader, with above-average athletic ability, I encountered Coaches Rhodes and Clay very early in my first year of high school. These individuals were in many ways contrasts to each other. Coach Rhodes, a Caucasian man in his mid-fifties, served as head basketball coach during the week and a farmer on the weekend. Coach Clay, an African American man in his early thirties, served as the assistant varsity coach. Both had outstretched hands and I grew as an athlete and a young man.

My father, who was serving as the chief financial officer and graduate professor at Morgan State University, advanced in his career at the end of my junior year in high school when he accepted his first college presidency. I was identified as the starting center on the basketball team at Wilde Lake High School, so a decision had to be made. Would my mother and I remain in Columbia for the completion of my senior year, or would we relocate to a new home in Schenectady, New York?

Once again the influence of my father came to the fore. He arranged for my mother and me to make a series of exploratory visits to Schenectady. On one such visit he had arranged for me to visit the high school in the community of Niskayuna, where we would live. He had told the principal about me being an outstanding student and also a promising basketball player. With that advance "intelligence," when he took me to the high school they rolled out the red carpet for me and the decision was made. I said "yes," I will relocate and would also play in the unofficial summer basketball league. Once again, there was the confluence of family and others in a positive way.

My father and I had a unique bonding experience for three and a half months as the school year began. My mother had remained in Maryland to handle the sale of our home there, and he and I lived in the YMCA residential facility that was across the street from his college. We did everything together for that period. I must say that our closeness rose to a new level because of having the YMCA as our temporary home. He was the first African American president of a college in the State University of New York System, so he made quite a "splash" with his entry into the community. I also made a similar impact because I was installed as the starting center on the basketball team, and we were winning games. He and I would compare our "credits" as they appeared in the local newspapers.

My high school experience was notable in that my academic and athletic pattern and success continued. I was heavily recruited and my parents and I visited numerous colleges when I had been invited. I wanted to be in a strong academic community where I could also play basketball. My father was a strong influence in causing me to choose to attend LeMoyne College in Syracuse over Brown University. Because of that decision, I became a four-year starter as center on the basketball team, entered the 1,000 point club, and amassed an impressive record as chemistry major.

Fast forward to the present, I am the Chief Executive Officer of an urban healthcare system in Northern California. My system has the dubious distinction of being the recipient of the rampant hopelessness that exists in many East San Francisco Bay communities. As a safety net hospital, a community's dependency manifests itself in patients whose physical bodies and spirits have been ravaged by street and domestic violence, homelessness, substance abuse, and mental health disorders. One cannot help but mourn when the disintegration of the family unit, paired with the absence of spiritual centering, results in the dysfunction that is so prevalent in our society. As many "experts" have cited, much of this dysfunction can be traced to the lack of strong father figures, particularly in the African American community.

So as you peruse the pages in this collection of "wisdom," ponder on the following four questions to percolate your thoughts.

- What responsibility do I have to outstretch my hand in a way that leverages the lessons that I learned in my life, and that builds strength in others, particularly the African American males?
- Given what some would characterize as the current downward spiral of the African American male in U.S. society, what responsibility do I have to reverse the daunting trends

that create a sense of hopelessness in so many of our communities?

- What have I done to share my gifts and talents with those who could benefit most from my life experiences?
- If my answers to any of these questions reflect that I have not contributed fully, what will I commit to do differently?

It is my hope that this book will provide each reader with some pearls of wisdom, new tools, and rekindles the flame that burns inside each of us to contribute more broadly than just to our own success.

God bless . . .

FOR MEN

In his book, <u>Day by Day with Charles Swindoll</u>, (Nashville: W Publishing Group—2000) he makes a strong case for fathers to step up, take responsibility, and overcome temptations that they face. He offers cogent advice and we wanted to share it with those who choose to read this book.

"I don't often recommend a volume without reservation, but I think every man should read <u>Temptations Men Face</u> by Tom Eisenman. I'm not saying I agree with everything in it, or that you will, but his observations, insights, and suggestions are both penetrating and provocative. In fact, that book got me thinking about the top temptations fathers face."

"First, the temptation to give things instead of giving ourselves. Don't misunderstand. Providing for one's family is biblical. First Timothy 5:8 calls the man who fails to provide for his family's needs "worse than an unbeliever." But the temptation I'm referring to goes far beyond the basic level of need. It's the toys vs. time battle: a dad's desire to make up for his long hours and absences by unloading material stuff on his family rather than being there when he is needed."

"Second, the temptation to save our best for the workplace. How easy it is for dads to use up their energy, enthusiasm, humor, and zest for life at work, leaving virtually nothing for the end of the day."

"Third, the temptation to deliver lectures rather than earning respect by listening and learning. When things get out of hand at home, it's our normal tendency to reverse the order James 1:19 suggests. First, we get mad. Then we shout. Last, we listen. When that happens, we get tuned out."

"Fourth, the temptation to demand perfection from those under our roof. We fathers can be extremely unrealistic, can't we? Fathers are commanded not to exasperate their children (Ephesians 6:4)."

"Fifth, the temptation to find intimate fulfillment outside the bonds of monogamy. Thanks to our ability to rationalize, we men can talk ourselves into the most ridiculous predicaments imaginable."

"Sixth, the temptation to underestimate the importance of cultivating your family's spiritual appetite. Fathers, listen up! Your wife and kids long for you to be their spiritual pacesetter."

"Are you ready for a challenge? Begin to spend time with God, become a man of prayer, help your family know how deeply you love Christ and desire to honor Him."

"How about facing the music and then changing the tune? Say a firm NO to any of these subtle, sneaky, slippery temptations that have slipped into your life."[1]

---

1   This quotation was used with permission as it helps to put in perspective the messages that we seek to impart in this book.

PART II

POINTS ON MENTORING

THE ESSENTIALS OF BEING A MENTOR

- Is someone absolutely credible whose integrity transcends the message, be it positive or negative.

- Tells you the things you may not want to hear, but leaves you feeling you have been heard.

- Interacts with you in a way that makes you want to become better.

- Makes you feel secure enough to take risks.

- Gives you the confidence to rise above your inner doubts and fears.

- Supports your attempts to set stretch goals for yourself.

- Presents opportunities and highlights challenges you might not have seen on your own.

ARE YOU A MENTOR OR A TORMEN-TOR?

Concerning your spiritual life, every Christian is supposed to assume the role of a mentor. Jesus, in what we now call The Great Commission, told us, "Therefore go and make disciples of all nations" (Matt. 28:19). That's a lot of discipling. It's a lot of mentoring. And if we are not careful, it could mean a lot of tormenting.

What is the main difference between a mentor and a tormentor? A helpful illustration that I heard from a Salvation Army officer involves a trampoline. A tormentor uses his trainee as dead weight to steady the trampoline so that he himself can bounce more securely. However, anyone who has enjoyed a trampoline knows that two people bounce higher together than either could bounce alone.

These are the expectations of the mentor:

- Considers mentoring a privilege and a great opportunity for reciprocal sharing and learning.
- Makes training time a high priority. He is prepared for teaching time, overflowing with ideas to share.
- May be concerned about being overzealous in the amount of training and experiences planned.
- Expects to minister to the trainee, setting the example in prayer, devotions and counsel.
- Defends his trainee and accepts blame when a program or project does not turn out as expected.
- Seeks to share every aspect of the position including weaknesses, failures and hurts.

- Uses criticism constructively with an encouraging effect: "That was good; add this or subtract that and it will be even better."
- Seek to find a trainee's "making point"—what motivates and inspires him or her—then fans the flame. Being a mentor also involves identifying and building upon the best there is in an individual.

You may agree that this seems achievable in theory, but unrealistic in practice. Some people are easier to mentor than others. In some cases the <u>mentor</u> ends up being the one tormented. You may ask yourself, is it really possible to apply this information in all situations?

I can think of no more mismatched group of people than the disciples of Jesus. He worked with individuals who were at least as difficult to mentor as any today. Yet even in the bleakest of situations, He never stooped to torment them.

It is easy to accept our current standards as appropriate for mentoring. But who sets the standard? Do we, or does Jesus? We must strive to be a model mentor and not a tormentor.

ROLE MODELS

The basketball legend Michael Jordan had some sage advice regarding role models. He said in <u>A New Man</u> magazine interview, "I want to encourage parents to be close knit and there for their children every day. That's where kids should find role models. It's parents who should discipline their kids . . . and if parents aren't there, maybe there's a coach, or someone else who's there on a day-to-day basis, who has values."

The NBA legend closed the interview with the comment: "It all starts with God."

Sound too simplistic? Maybe to some. But when a celebrity the status of Michael Jordan recognizes that it's God we need, perhaps those who don't normally pay too much attention to such advice should sit up and take notice.

Being a positive influence on someone doesn't come down to how much money you make, all the toys you can accumulate, all the fancy clothes you can wear or all the exotic and adventurous places you've visited. Being a role model takes time, devotion, integrity, consistency, commitment and a great deal of love. It starts at square one—having a personal relationship with the living God.

Putting God first will not only bring peace to your life but will also allow you to be a positive influence on those around you. "Come follow me," says Jesus Christ, the ultimate role model. "I am the way, the truth and the life."

THE FLAXEN SHIRT

The first seventeen years of my professional life were spent at Tuskegee Institute in Alabama. Tuskegee was founded by the famed educator, Booker T. Washington. Anyone who spends an extended period of service at that institution will become intimately familiar with historical footnotes.

Booker T. Washington, in his autobiography, Up From Slavery, remembered his boyhood days as a slave in Virginia.

Among the many unpleasant features of those days were the flaxen shirts worn by slaves. The roughest, cheapest part of the flax was used for the slave garments. As a result, the coarse shirts scratched and pricked the wearers until frequent washings and constant wearing had broken them in.

Often, Washington remembered, when it came time for a new shirt for him, his older brother John would wear the shirt and endure the pain and itching until it had softened with many wearings. Then he would return it to his brother, Booker, who in that way was delivered from the suffering his burden would have caused.

There is an important teaching principle contained in the example of John and Booker Washington.

How much more has Jesus carried your burden and borne your pain? How much more has He suffered for you, in your place? "Surely he took up our infirmities and carried our sorrows . . . he was pierced for our transgressions, he was crushed for our iniquities . . . We all, like sheep, have gone astray, each of us has turned in his own way; and the Lord has laid on him the iniquity of us all" (Isaiah 53:4-6).

Turn to Jesus today, and let His love and sacrifice be your salvation.

THERE IS A RIVER

I ask you, how long shall we suffer inequities and injustices in this country? How long must the children suffer? How long shall there be a need for affirmative action programs? When will we be able to live, truly, as brothers and sisters?

Recall for a moment the picture before Ezekiel the Prophet. He was shown a river. "The man measured a thousand cubits, and then led me through the water, and it was ankle-deep."

"Again he measured a thousand cubits and led me through the water and it was knee-deep. Again he measured a thousand cubits and led me through the water and it was up to the loins. Again, he measured a thousand and it was a river that I could not pass through, for the water had risen."

Indeed the water is rising. Frederick Douglass said, "If there is no struggle, there is no progress. Those who profess to favor freedom, and yet deprecate agitation are men who want crops without plowing up the ground. They want the rain without thunder and lightning. They want the ocean without the awful roar of its many waters . . ." Can you hear the roar?

There is a river in America. A river whose source is from on high. These waters are filled with the lives of great Black men and women of fortitude and achievement. Dreamers and schemers are they, who chiseled out a life in this wilderness/promised land. Committed to freedom and dignity they sprang forth from the holy place.

There is a river in America. A river whose course is shaping the destiny of this country. Transportation, food, industry, and recreation all depend on this river. Without the river, the land would be barren. A necessity of life, this river must be respected. This river tolerates no obstacles.

There is a river in America. A river whose force though mighty has been underrated. Daily the momentum grows as enlightened souls join the waters uniting in streams of truth and justice for all.

Oh yes, the current in this river is swift and the riverbed is deep. But it is these very waters that heal the land.

Yes, I see W.E.B. DuBois and Mary McLeod Bethune. Athletes, actors, and astronauts. Maids and musicians, ministers, too. Teachers, public servants, and business servants. All these are in the river—they heal our land. Some with hands sore and scarred from the work they have done. Others with broken backs or spilled blood. Every drop of water in that river is straight from the heart of God.

There is a river in America. A river whose power is the spirit of a people. A spirit that will not be broken!

Can you hear it roar?

THE TEN COMMANDMENTS OF HOW TO GET ALONG WITH PEOPLE

1. Keep skid chains on your tongue. Always say less than you think. Cultivate a low, persuasive voice. How you say it often counts more than what you say.
2. Make promises sparingly, and keep them faithfully, no matter what it costs you.
3. Never let an opportunity pass to say a kind and encouraging word to or about somebody. Praise good work, regardless of who did it. If criticism is needed, criticize helpfully, never spitefully.
4. Be interested in others, their pursuits, and their work, their homes and families. Make merry with those who rejoice, with those who weep, with those who mourn. Let everyone you meet, however humble, feel that you regard him or her as a person of importance.
5. Be cheerful. Don't burden or depress those around you by dwelling on your minor aches and pains and small disappointments. Remember that everyone is carrying some kind of a load.
6. Keep an open mind. Discuss but don't argue. It is a mark of a superior mind to be able to disagree without being disagreeable.
7. Let your virtues, if you have any, speak for themselves. Refuse to talk of another's vices. Discourage gossip. It is a waster of valuable time and can be extremely destructive.
8. Be careful of another's feelings. Wit and humor at the other person's expense are rarely worth it and may even hurt when least expected.

9. Pay no attention to ill-natured remarks about you. Remember that the person who carried the message may not be the most accurate reporter in the world. Simply live so that nobody will believe them. Disordered nerves and bad digestion are a common cause of backbiting.
10. Don't be too anxious about the credit due you. Do your best, and be patient. Forget about yourself, and let others "remember." Success is much sweeter that way.

FOOD FOR THOUGHT

⊞ Success is just a matter of luck. Ask any failure.

⊞ Some people drink from the fountain of knowledge. Others just gargle.

⊞ In order to change, we must be sick and tired of being sick and tired.

⊞ Moving fast is not the same as going somewhere.

⊞ An atheist is a person with no invisible means of support.

⊞ The only thing you have no choice about is making choices.

⊞ Your past is always going to be the way it was, stop trying to change it.

⊞ When your dreams turn to dust, take out the vacuum cleaner.

⊞ The only true authority figure is within yourself.

⊞ When the going gets tough everyone leaves.

— Unknown Source

TO MY GROWN-UP SON

My hands were busy through the day,
I didn't have much time to play
The little games you asked me to.
I didn't have much time for you.
I'd wash your clothes, I'd sew and cook,
But when you'd bring your picture book
And ask me, please, to share your fun,
I'd say, "A little later, Son."

I'd tuck you in all safe at night,
And hear your prayers, turn out the light,
Then tiptoe softly to the door.

I wish I'd stayed a minute more.
For life is short, and years rush past,
A little boy grown up so fast.
No longer is he at your side,
His precious secrets to confide.

The picture books are put away.
There are no children's games to play,
No good-night kiss, no prayers to hear.
That all belongs to yesteryear.
My hands once busy, now lie still
The days are long and hard to fill.
I wish I might go back and do
The little things you asked me to.

— Source: Unknown

THE THREE THINGS REMINDER
FOR FATHERS

- Three things in life that, once gone, never come back.
    1. Time
    2. Words
    3. Opportunity

- Three things in life that may never be lost.
    1. Peace
    2. Hope
    3. Honesty

- Three things in life that are most valuable.
    1. Love
    2. Self-confidence
    3. Friends

- Three things in life that are never certain.
    1. Dreams
    2. Success
    3. Fortune

- Three things in life that make a person.
    1. Hard work
    2. Sincerity
    3. Commitment

- Three things in life that can destroy a person.
    1. Alcohol and drugs
    2. Pride

3. Anger

▦ Three things in life that are truly constant.
   1. Father
   2. Son
   3. Holy Ghost

I ask the Lord to bless you, as I pray for you today, to guide you and protect you, as you go along your way. God's love is always with you. God's promises are true. And when you give God all your cares, you know that God will see you through.

THE BANQUET

Ask! What is your goal when you are leading people?
What is the Center of You?

If at the center of you is yourself –
Prepare to be lonely.

If at the center of you, you plan to gain power –
Forget affection.

If at the center of you is security –
Forget ecstasy.

If you seek justice without mercy –
Don't make any mistakes.

If your life is quantitative –
You better keep up your averages.

If your life is a rat race –
Forget dignity.

If your life is centered around manipulation –
Don't expect people to trust you.

If you are a gossip –
Don't look for confidences.

If you are materialistic –
Forget spiritual values.

If you are confrontational –
Don't expect tenderness when you need it.

If you decide to live by the sword –
Then by God you better carry one.

Do you know <u>why</u> to all of the above?
Life is moral. We really do reap what we sow.

Everyone, sooner or later, gets to sit down to a banquet of
consequences –

<u>What Will You Eat At Your Banquet</u>?

A MAN'S DREAM

A man dreamed that he was at home alone, and as the day wore on he began to hear voices in the basement. Eventually he went down to investigate and discovered a man working in a basement office. From the equipment in the room and the drawings that were around, it was obvious the man was an architect. As he conversed with him, he revealed that he was the architect of this man's house. The man not only expressed surprise that he was the designer of the house, but also that he had been oblivious to the fact that someone had an office in his basement. The architect told him that there was something else, which he had not known.

There were more rooms in his house than he had explored. The architect gave him a tour. He opened door after door, showing him rooms he had not known were there. The most striking thing remembered about the room was that there were no walls, no limits, and no boundaries. <u>Then the dream ended</u>.

That dream is representative of each of us. The house is each of us. The architect, the designer of the space is God. The message is that God has created many more rooms in the house than we are aware of—rooms without limits.

Are you and the architect walking together as you explore the rooms without walls? That is how men, women, boys and girls, all of us can be involved in the building of a better Church, and a better life. May God be with us all in this endeavor.

WHAT IS SO ADULT ABOUT OBSCENITY?

I am daily dismayed with the language that I hear used by people on the streets of our cities and in various media forms. I get tired of hearing obscene language described as "adult language" and pornographic films called "adult movies." What's so adult about obscenity?

I am certainly not advocating that someone be marched into court for swearing when he drops a hammer on his toe. But I question whether there's anything adult about most of the things we describe as <u>adult</u>.

Swearing is so much a part of life today that it is taken for granted. Obscene literature is regarded as liberated. Pornographic movies symbolize a free society.

As far as I'm concerned, being an adult should mean having some knowledge and a sense of responsibility. It should also mean that we've learned to consider other people's feelings. It should also mean we have learned to express ourselves clearly in a language that is one of our richest heritages.

It's unfortunate that some of the fine old elements of our language have been so misused for so long that they have become useless for their original purposes.

Listen to some conversations among young people, then ask yourselves how often the most famous four-letter word, and three-letter word is used correctly—or even in a way that is anatomically possible—and you'll comprehend what I mean.

I agree that words that stand for natural bodily functions and for acts of love should never have become regarded as synonymous with obscenities. But it's too late to rescue them now.

Our only choice, if we want both to make ourselves understood and not to give offense, is to stop using those terms. There's nothing adult about using them. Rather, it smacks of young boys who are trying to shock others.

It's often used unintentionally, but it cannot fail to have an effect on anyone who believes in God. Usually it will make a Christian feel sad that the other person obviously has no idea of who Jesus is.

Because of my physical stature, and the fact that I am both a college president and a preacher, I have walked up to a group of people who have been using fairly ordinary obscenities and seen them become nervous and apologetic when they've noticed me.

"Jesus Christ, pastor," "I am sorry Mr. President," they say. The truth is, however, that I can cope with hearing the name of my Savior used without thought or reverence.

Being adult includes respecting other people and their beliefs. For that reason, there is nothing adult about blasphemy. Most of it may be thoughtless rather than intended. But there is nothing adult about being thoughtless, either!

A TRUE FRIENDSHIP

Even at my stage in life as a senior citizen, I relish reading the comic strip—"Dennis the Menace." Watching the escapes of Dennis being the bane of the existence of Mr. Wilson brings joy to my life.

Over a decade ago I rushed to the theater when Hank Ketcham's popular strip character came to the big screen in "Dennis."

In the film, as with the original comic strip and TV series that preceded it in the 1950s and 60s, the boy doesn't really mean to cause havoc—it's just the inevitable result of his enthusiastic explorations. Mishap and a little mischief are his constant companions.

True to form, poor old neighbor George Wilson bears the brunt of Dennis' guileless chaos.

But what's the plot? This is where the sinister "Switchblade Sam" comes on the scene. Sam makes friends with Dennis and his pals to find out as much as he can about their parent's houses, which he plans to rob. He's tolerant of the children's antics because he needs to stay on good terms with them.

Mr. Wilson, on the other hand, appears to suffer desperately at the hands of young Dennis. His most strenuous daily activity seems to be exercising patience with the little boy whom he secretly admires for his energy and his ingenuity. While the Mr. Wilson character appears gruff and intolerant, he has a warm heart. He really likes the boy next door and has the little guy's best interests in mind.

I suppose the moral of this tale is quite simple: some people only appear to be good friends. They indulge us, ignoring or even encouraging our small misdemeanors, believing their approval of our lifestyle will win our trust and friendship.

Sadly, these tactics work all too well and many of us are taken in by "smooth operators" whose real motive is to use other people, then drop them afterwards.

So be aware of false friends. Try instead to cultivate a relation-ship with Jesus Christ, the one true friend who knows each of us better than anyone else does—and still loves us!

FINDING HAPPINESS—THE TRUTH

<u>The Flintstones</u>, the "modern Stone Age family" that captured the imaginations of viewers when the show first appeared on prime time TV in the early '60s, came back over a decade ago (1995), that time in a live-action, full-length film.

<u>The Flintstones</u> took us back to the happy town of Bedrock, two million B.C., where foot-driven cars rumble past split-level caves and every kitchen comes complete with a pig-powered garbage disposal unit.

Part slapstick and part social satire, the original television version—the first cartoon sitcom—poked fun at contemporary suburban life as it followed the antics of Fred and Wilma Flintstone, a Stone Age working-class couple, and their family and friends in Bedrock.

In the full-length film the cartoon was brought to life by real actors and actresses. According to film producer Bruce Cohen, "There is something of the Flintstones in all of us. They represent the traditional American couple who believe in family, and want to better themselves so they can make a nicer life for themselves, their children and their friends. With that background, we created our conflict—that Fred is lured by the trappings of success."

Certainly Fred is not alone in being tempted to find ways of getting rich quick. Most parents would like to provide more for their children. And there's nothing wrong with being wealthy.

The danger comes when the acquisition of money or possessions takes too high a priority in life. It's no fun being poor, but wealth is no guarantee of happiness. Unbelievable though it may seem to those who have to watch the balance in their account at the end of the month, miserable millionaires are by no means an endangered species.

When multi-millionaire J. Paul Getty lay on his deathbed, someone asked, "How much did he leave?" A friend replied—"Everything."

In The Flintstones, Fred discovers that pursuing wealth is no sure way of finding happiness. It's a truth as old as time.

Sometimes we too often get diverted by "things." Get-rich-quick is just one of them. Fame and power can be other distractions from the real joy of living.

Jesus asked, "What shall it profit a man, if he shall gain the whole world, and lose his own soul?" (Mark 8:36).

It's a good question for us today. By trusting Jesus as your personal Savior you can have the life-changing answer.

THE DEDICATED BLACK MEN
OF JASPER COUNTY

Three years ago on one of our trips to the family vacation home on Hilton Head Island, South Carolina, we came to know about the Dedicated Black Men of Jasper County. This is a group formed as a result of an informal survey conducted by Leroy Sneed. He asked Jasper County middle and high school boys what they wanted to be when they grew up. He found that the answers almost always followed one of two dreams: professional athlete or rap star.

As he was not happy with those answers he gathered a few of his colleagues and friends, successful men who had owned businesses and raised families. They formed the Dedicated Black Men of Jasper County and decided to go to the schools to show the students tangible, local examples of success. The group's founder, Leroy Sneed, said "I wanted to help black young men."

When they come to the schools, they dress in suits and ties. They encourage the students to look them in the eye when addressing them. They share stories of how they were just like them, living in rural areas, but how they worked hard to be successful.

Who are these men? They are managers, principals, contractors, teachers, political figures and entrepreneurs, many of whom live in nice houses and drive nice cars. One even worked his way up from washing cars to owning several car dealerships in the Low Country area.

Marion Burns is another member of the group. He says, "You can see the gleam in their eyes. Even though we are in the 21st century, it's hard to believe that the majority of these kids don't have a broad scope of career opportunities. We're pointing out other possibilities for them."

Burns is a resident of Bluffton, South Carolina who is retired from the insurance business. He and Sneed are members of the eight-person contingent, all successful and from the Lowcountry, who have been going to Jasper County High School, Ridgeland Middle School and West Hardeeville School for the past two years. They speak to boys who typically are labeled "at-risk" by school counselors or social workers. But Burns thinks that all the students need is guidance.

They admit that some of the boys are academically challenged and others have discipline problems. They have found that what is needed are good role models to encourage the students in not just their career paths, but in their character development.

But the role models many black youths look up to today are the ones who make millions playing professional football and basketball. Some young people even admire drug dealers because they, too, make a lot of money. They tell the boys that those paths are dangerous to follow.

So the <u>Dedicated Black Men of Jasper County</u> try to emulate what a good role model should be. Growing up, these men had a different kind of role model to look up to than youth do today, they say. As you talk to the men they tell you about the teachers and other men in Jasper County who were making a difference by taking a stand during the American civil rights movement.

The example of Leroy Sneed is one which can be emulated in other communities across this nation as we seek to reverse the trend of so many black men and youth being incarcerated.

Sneed is a semi-retired barber who has a history of "doing for others." He recruited other blacks in the community to register to vote in the 1960s and he also helped to integrate the local political system. He served on the Jasper County Council for more than 12 years.

Drawing on his own experiences in growing up, he started the group of dedicated black men in hopes of teaching Lowcountry area youth who were starting to fall by the wayside. He wanted to give them the push they needed to be good, productive citizens.

They perform their work of enlightenment by inviting the boys to go on group trips to their homes and businesses, telling them and showing them they can achieve their dreams by getting an education.

The comments of Dayne Wright, a promising young 17-year old participant, are instructive. He still has ambitions of being a professional football player, but he knows he will need a fallback plan if the dream does not pan out.

"I'll be a professional counselor for I like talking to people and stuff."

This rising Jasper County High School senior was deeply impressed with the mentor group and the lifestyle that some of them lived. "One lived in a plantation—like a two-story house and he drives nice cars. I want to have all that stuff too."

Leroy Sneed, Marion Burns, Henry C. Lawson and Isiah Toomer are mature men who grew up in Jasper County. They have made a difference and they continue to make a difference through the Dedicated Black Men of Jasper County organization. This is a model that should be widely emulated. All it takes is a few dedicated black men.

The Dedicated Black Men of Jasper County - Part II

Part II of this essay is being penned as my wife and I are on Hilton Head Island for a two-week vacation, and I wanted to follow up on the work of the Dedicated Black Men of Jasper County.

In talking with the editor of the local newspaper, The Island Packet, I learned that this project has brought a much-needed dose of reality to the new generation. "The project members are urging today's young men to aspire to decent, fruitful lives that are much more down to earth than those of the sports and pop culture stars they see constantly splashed across the screen. They are urging the young men not to ruin their lives with drugs or the false gold of drug dealing. They are urging the young men to get ahead the old fashioned way, through an education and hard work."

The editor continued: "Statistically, the Dedicated Black Men of Jasper County face an impossible challenge. Members look around and see poverty as low as it gets in America. They see public schools drastically below state achievement levels and not in the same ballpark of national expectations. They see high dropout rates. They see too few intact families, with most young men missing a father figure in the home. They see an environment where black men are more likely than most to end up in jail, or shot, or both."

Those are daunting comments from the editor, for they could be repeated in many other communities—Dallas and Oakland being no exception.

But the encouraging fact is that the Dedicated Black Men of Jasper County have themselves crossed the same gauntlets. They were reared in the same rural, poor county with little opportunity and signs of failure all around. But each of them rose above those circumstances and they present themselves to the boys that they are mentoring that "you can do likewise."

What the young men of Jasper County and Dallas and Oakland should hear is the following statement from The Black Star Project in Chicago, now organizing its "Million Father March" into the schools on the first day of school this year: "When fathers are involved in the educational lives of their children, children earn better grades, get higher test scores, enjoy school more, and are more likely to graduate from high school and attend college. Encouraging men to become more active in the lives of their children does not mean that mothers are not doing a good job. However, statistics show that a good parent team is more effective raising children than a single parent, whether the single parent is a man or a woman."

This is not to say that success has not come from a single-parent family. However any single head of a family will tell you how difficult it was. It has been my experience in Dallas that the single mother welcomes a respected male influence in the lives of their boys.

The young men of Jasper County, and other communities, also need to hear that they can take advantage of the suffering forced on their grandfathers and great-grandfathers. They should hear that in today's corporate world, African-Americans are highly sought as companies struggle to diversify the work force. Not only are African Americans sometimes begged to come on board, but they are highly sought in management positions.

All that I have shared is a fact of life, and young men of Jasper County and elsewhere should aspire to gain the social and academic skills to fill positions in varied walks of professional life. African Americans can have a leg up if they will do the work and seize the opportunity.

Success does not happen instantly, and it takes a lot of hard work. The Dedicated Black Men of Jasper County volunteers are to be commended for telling it like it is. There should be many more replications across this nation's landscape.

GREAT EXPECTATIONS

I am a post-depression era child, who was born, and spent my formative and young adult years in the segregated society that existed in this nation at that time. My parents were both drop-outs from high school who were married just before what would have been their senior year in high school. They had no marketable skills, but they were ambitious. Being the oldest of nine children, I saw first-hand how they labored to craft a life for themselves and their children. It was difficult for them, but they persisted and scaled very challenging mountains during a difficult period in the life of this nation.

In spite of the limitations and privations associated with living during the era of raw and unquestioned segregation, I took to heart the values they exhibited of self-confidence, hard work, thrift, faith, and the power of education. Let me add at this juncture in this little essay that although my parents were initially high-school dropouts, they both subsequently earned baccalaureate degrees, and my father earned a master's degree and was awarded an honorary doctorate. They valued and treasured the worth of education.

My mother taught me how to read at age 3 by placing me in the bed with her on Sundays where she would teach me to read using comic books. At age 5 she enrolled me in a "private school." It was in the home of Mrs. Chavis and we would view it in today's environment as simply a daycare center. But I always remembered her as a wonderful teacher. Upon the completion of my first year under her tutelage she informed my mother that I had successfully completed the work of the first year of school and that I should be advanced to the second grade when I enrolled in public school. As this was an unrecognized school, my mother resisted and I began public school in the first grade. It was her view that I now had a firm foundation for success in school. Although disappointed, I came to recognize, in later years, that my mother was planting the seeds of great expectations.

The only person in our family who had ever attended college when I was about to graduate from high school was an aunt. As was the practice during that era, she attended a state college on Saturdays and during the summers until she finally earned her bachelor's degree. She, along with my parents, instilled in all of us that we would attend and graduate from college. Thus, the seeds of expectation were now being fertilized and deepened.

My father had an expression that I share in encounters with young people even today—"If you want to get ahead, get something in your head." And so it was that today, although my parents have gone to their eternal home, their children took the lessons to heart. Of the nine children, eight have advanced degrees, and five earned the doctorate. In my case I have multiple earned doctorates. And it all started with seeds planted early and with the mantra—"If you want to get ahead, get something in your head."

Recounting my family history, in miniature, was only for the purpose of perspective. Today some communities have heard first-hand the exhortations from Bill Cosby on the role of parents in causing their children to have high aspirations. He admonishes parents and parent-figures to work even harder to cause their children to have "great expectations," in spite of the challenges of contemporary life. While his admonishments have brought criticism in some circles, even from African Americans, one has to acknowledge the importance of our young people learning the value of self-confidence, education, goal-setting and expectations at the earliest possible age.

In a recent issue of Fortune magazine there was an interesting article on the subject of great expectations written by John Elliott. His short article was included in this special issue of the magazine that addressed the question—"Can Americans Compete?"

In responding to the question—"What kind of global competition does your kid face?" he shared with readers how teenagers in India have big ambitions and the confidence to match.

He begins by describing 15-year old Saksham Karwal as "smart and creative as any American over-achievers you're likely to meet, and maybe a little more driven." The young man describes himself as "We have the best brains, and we can beat anyone—no one is ahead of us."

This young man comes from a family where his father is a former top executive at a multinational appliance manufacturing company. Karwal wants to go to one of the elite Indian Institutes of Technology (ITT) to study engineering, then get an MBA and join a "good company."

He then describes a young man at the other end of the spectrum. Amar Nath is 17 and has never been to a conventional school and has just started learning to read and write—but he has the same drive as Karwal. After "high class people" in a Delhi market, where he was a porter, Nath realized that "speaking their English was a basic driving force." His "great expectations" have caused him to want to start his own hotel or restaurant, and benefit from the growing consumerism in India.

Elliott offers that these two young boys are not unusual or unique. Both of them reflect the self-confidence of India's youth that has grown exponentially since the country's economy began to open up 14 years ago. That has given them the incentive to work toward achieving their goals. Additionally, both of the young men acknowledge the existence of the insecurity of not having a safety net of any kind in India. He quotes the young boys thusly: "In the U.S. the government provides for unemployment and Social Security, there is nothing here."

The two boys also feel relentless parental pressure. Their parents set strict goals, and as a result they feel that they must succeed.

Their schools are demanding and there is a heavy focus on grades and success. Even in India, that focus can be excessive. Stories about students nervously waiting for exam results are widely reported, as are suicides by those overwhelmed by the pressure. But the students are quick to assert that "the strong survive, and if you try, you will succeed."

In our nation, and particularly in the African American communities, we need to instill those core values in the young people. They must be taught that you can survive; you can gain strength; you can succeed—if you will try.

Dr. Wright L. Lassiter, Jr.

WHATEVER HAPPENED TO LOVE?

It was one of the young boys that I mentor who brought it up. He bought himself one of the latest in music players and he's into the "new sounds."

But he's not impressed with the emphasis of a lot of today's songs.

He argues that songs of my day are better than new releases. Not just because of the quality of the 60's music. "The old songs talk about love. The new ones don't get past sex," he says.

"They talk about wanting somebody's body or going to bed with someone. The old songs included more thought than that. Naturally, they included the suggestion of sex, but they spoke about love."

I can see what he means. A glance at today's pop videos, the DVD's, television—forget the words for a minute—show where the emphasis is.

Hard, seductive looks. Writhing bodies waiting for fulfillment. Lots of skin as you look at the low-cut jeans, exposed midriffs, and tight fits. Tantalizing poses and "prove you can do it" stares.

They ooze sex. They miss out on love. He continues, "Our generation isn't getting a fair deal. We're having all this pumped out at us without any intelligent reference to what sex is about." "It's no wonder a lot of my pals are mixed up. Nobody's telling them about love."

His generation is getting a raw deal. They're being exploited. Sensationalizing sex brings money. Sex is exciting. It makes people curious. It can be like a drug.

A young, gullible public is easily caught. They're even fooled into thinking they've just invented sex—and previous generations knew nothing about it.

Is there any hope for love? Of course there is! We can't survive without it. We have to return to loving relationships to get some stability for living.

But an awful lot of people are getting hurt along the way. They're learning by their mistakes.

Sex without love isn't new, but it misses the point. Sex within a life-long, loving, faithful commitment finds its true meaning.

One more thing. We all need help to understand what true love is. God has shown us through Jesus Christ how deep love can be. How selfless. How complete.

I wish today's generation knew more about that.

Dr. Wright L. Lassiter, Jr.

BATMAN ISN'T INNOCENT—OK?

In 1990 Batman hit the world scene. Batman is here. All's right with the world. The Cape Crusader is in control of Gotham City—and the world's press—and the box offices—and our pockets. Batman is back!

Batman has really zapped it to us. He has "ker-powed" the American public to the tune of 600 million dollars in the first few weeks of the film's showing.

Actor Jack Nicholson, the Joker, is said to be raking in a cool 30 million from the sale of Batman artifacts and paraphernalia.

What about Batman himself? Well, this Michael Keaton character is a little earthier than the too-good-to-be-true Adam West television character. His halo has definitely slipped. But all that helps box-office receipts soar to the highest ever.

So Batman has out-zapped James Bond, Superman and the entire Star Wars crew in one fell swoop.

He's said to be more in keeping with author Bob Kane's original 1939 character. So much so that the film has been given a PG 13 rating (parental guidance for children under 13).

So it's fantasy time for the adults. Escapism for the grown-ups. They've kicked the kiddies out and taken over their make-believe world. And with it has gone the innocence of the old films.

Innocence has to be replaced by reality sooner or later. For kids in today's celluloid world it's sooner. They will be watching the new version on their videos before you can say Jack Nicholson.

When reality dawns, when people are seen for the sometimes less-than-perfect, two-timing, dastardly, cynical creatures they can be, it isn't any use calling on Batman—old or new version—to put things right. Life isn't like that.

Even so, the new Batman has been brought down to earth to make him more convincing. Perhaps we, the big Batmania spenders, need to come down to earth too—because escapism is all right only if we spend most of our time in the real world fighting its real battles.

Batman's back, all's right with the world? We know that's not true.

The only person who really did come down to earth, Jesus Christ, God's son, is the only person who has actually confronted and defeated evil.

When the rest of us are ready to come down to earth, Jesus Christ has some work for us to do, to really make the world a better place—starting with ourselves.

PART III

PARENTS AND THEIR CHILDREN

WE CANNOT FAIL OUR BLACK CHILDREN

Last year marked the 50th anniversary of Brown vs. Board of Education, which theoretically ended public school segregation in our nation. All of us who spoke before groups during that period of commemoration remarked that many schools are as segregated today as they were before the ruling. We also spoke of Black children throughout the nation who are performing at the bottom of the American educational system.

In one talk I spoke of the paradox in Washington, D.C. and Prince George's County, Maryland. The Maryland community, which is almost 70 percent Black, is one of the most affluent Black communities in the nation. The paradox is strikingly this: It is also one of the lowest-performing counties in the entire state of Maryland!

An achievement gap gives way to an employability gap, an earnings gap, a health care gap, a life expectancy gap, a housing gap, an incarceration gap, a marriage-capacity gap, a wealth gap, and other quality-of-life gaps. Research confirms that this achievement gap begins before children start school, widens between kindergarten and second grade, and is locked in by the third grade. The gap persists through elementary school, high school, college, and ultimately the workforce. The gap causes many Black people to be permanently "locked out."

Without a good education, many Black children are being prepared for the streets, the drug culture, violence, unemployment, prison and death. I am distressed when I hear young people state that their "hope in life" is to live to be age 18!

Black children will be unable to compete with the best and brightest students from all parts of the world for jobs in America. Without a good education, Black children are not much better off than the slaves that they might be studying about during Black History Month.

While the achievement gap is a difficult problem to solve, it can be solved. The key to fixing the problem is ensuring that Black parents, and parent-figures, are active, invested, and involved in the educational lives of their children.

Our Black children must be re-inspired and motivated to do well in school. Many Black students have simply turned away from education as they decry the so-called "nerds." Additionally, there must be equity in funding, school resources, class size, teacher quality, and other factors needed to educate Black children. There are gross disparities in those areas.

The parent-teacher connection that is directly related to improved student performance and high achievement must be strengthened. In addition, the overall Black community must develop and maintain high academic standards for all Black children—starting as soon as they are born into this world.

As leaders and concerned citizens we must raise the consciousness of the nation to the imperative that the education of Black children—all children—must become a priority. I am not a fan of slogans, however the slogan—"No Child Left Behind"—has strong merit.

While many individuals and institutions have a powerful role to play in reversing this problem, the Black community must supply the leadership. This thought must be embraced with vigor—"If not us, who?" Yes, the government must provide the financial resources and the legislative will, but we must provide the social capital through our commitment and our energy. We must have the "will."

The failure of Black children to be educated in American schools must be placed solely at their feet. We, as adults, share in the dilemma and the blame. And it will take all of us to fix this problem—before it is too late!

Dr. Wright L. Lassiter, Jr.

TAKE THE TELEVISION SET OUT OF THE BEDROOM

Children who watch a lot of television and have a set in the bedroom do significantly worse at school than others and are less likely to enter higher education institutions according to recently released research studies.

A series of studies published by scientists in New Zealand found that those who watched the most television were the least likely to leave school with qualifications for higher education and had a smaller chance of earning a university degree.

In another independent project, conducted by researchers at Stanford and Johns Hopkins universities, the results attest that children who had televisions in their rooms were found to be lower academic achievers. Those without a bedside TV, but who had access to a computer at home, did significantly better at mathematics, reading and language tests than their peers.

A third study, by researchers at the University of Washington in Seattle, found that television could impair the development of very young pre-school children, but may have some benefits for those aged between three and five.

The three studies appeared in <u>Archives of Pediatric and Adolescent Medicine</u>, a journal published by the American Medical Association. An accompanying editorial said that parents should choose with care programs that stimulate and are appropriate to the age of their children.

The New Zealand team, led by Robert Hancox, from the University of Otago, conducted a long-term study of more than 1,000 children aged 5, 7, 9, 11, 13 and 15. "The results of this study indicate that increased time spent watching television during childhood and adolescence was associated with a lower level of educational attainment by early adulthood," the authors concluded. "Lower mean viewing hours between 5 and 11 years of age were a stronger predictor of achieving a university degree."

The Stanford study followed a diverse group of almost 400 third-grade pupils, with an average age of eight, at six California schools. Children with a television set in their bedrooms, but no home computer, achieved the worse scores in school achievement tests. Those in the reverse situation scored the highest.

Thomas Robinson, from the Lucile Packard Children's Hospital at Stanford, who led the research said: "This study provides even more evidence that parents should take the television out of their child's room, or not put it there in the first place." The researchers, who found that more than 70 percent of pupils reported having a television in their bedroom, did not know why it had such an effect on examination results.

Dr. Robinson who has done previous studies showing that decreasing a child's time in front of the TV can reduce obesity, aggressive behavior and pestering of parents for advertised toys, added that it fitted with a pattern of behavior. "A television in a child's bedroom has become the norm," he said. "From the parent's perspective, it keeps the child amused and out of trouble. But with this arrangement, parents are giving up any control over how much and what their children are watching."

"They have no idea if they are watching all night, or if they are watching violent or sexually explicit content, or content or advertising that promotes alcohol or drug use."

The third study analyzed data on 1,797 children from a survey of mathematics, reading and comprehension skills. Frederick Zimmerman and Dimitri Christakis, from the University of Washington at Seattle, reported "a consistent pattern of negative associations between television, before age three years and adverse cognitive outcomes at ages six and seven years."

The results of these three studies should be instructive for parents and family members as they work to develop children effectively.

As we have sought to impress in other essays and selections in this book, choices are pivotal in an environment of sea change that we all experience.

TOO MANY CHOICES

Neighborhood watch has taken on a new meaning. Peeking out from our curtains doesn't only mean we're looking out for our neighbor's interests. We're also looking out for those who've just acquired new satellite television dishes!

Cable television presents more of a problem for those who like to speculate on their neighbor's lifestyles. With nothing as visible as a satellite dish it's not so easy to spot those who've opted for virtually unlimited choices in their television viewing.

Whether we're keen to monitor our neighbor's viewing habits from envy, or because we secretly despise those who need more than three television channels to keep them happy, is debatable.

In many households, war can break out over who is going to watch which channel, even with only three networks to choose from. How is a family to keep peace in multi-channel households? Perhaps people just shut themselves away with their own television set to watch programs of their choice in isolation.

Can there be too much choice on television? Will we turn into a nation of channel-hoppers, looking at a lot, but seeing very little?

Television has been described as an undifferentiated wilderness in which viewers aimlessly graze from one channel to the next, hardly noticing where they are.

Making choices between clear-cut options with clear-cut consequences is a relatively simple matter, even if we end up perversely making the wrong choice!

Adam and Eve knew all about that. Faced with the choice between obedience to God and disobedience, which carried a penalty of spoiling their relationship with God, they decided that the "forbidden fruit" of setting themselves up as equal with God was worth far more than their childlike dependence on Him.

What is your relationship with God like? Are you still channel hopping, or have you decided to serve Him?

STRESS AND THE HIGH SCHOOL SENIOR

The most stressful time for parents and their children is adolescence, from ages 12-19. Recently, two groups of high school seniors was asked by a researcher to list ways their parents try to cope with the young person's stressful situations.

The highest number of votes was given to what family therapists would consider inappropriate coping techniques. This was described in several ways, from "yelling at me" to "nagging" or "complaining constantly."

Nevertheless close on the heels of yelling was a very appropriate coping technique, namely, trying to talk through the teenager's stressful situation. However, to keep a discussion between parents and seniors one which does not look like a put-down for either adolescent or parent seems to be difficult to accomplish.

A close third for this researcher's informal poll were statements about parents who tried to be helpful—usually by giving advice.

A sizable number of students felt that their parents didn't care to deal with the adolescent's stressors. They reported that parents tried to ignore the situation by misuse of alcohol or drugs. Or they left teens to fend for themselves by going out, going to bed or ignoring the young person. And some parents seemed to worry so much about the student that they could no longer deal with their own anxieties.

Many students indicated a desire to discuss stressful situations with adults, possibly their parents, when such discussions would be meaningful for all concerned, and not the beginning of an argument. Some believed that their parents ignored them because they could not cope with their own problems, let alone those of their children.

In a few situations, students had been told to leave home or had been physically abused as the parent's way of coping with problems.

And in some families, parents were so "fed-up" with the students that they simply gave up and let the teen do whatever he or she wanted to do.

On a more positive note, a number of students mentioned that their parents showed them patience and an understanding of their limitations. In some instances, parents helped children with homework. Others allowed the young person to solve his stressors on his own and to make his own decision after listening to his parent's point of view. A few parents helped out by lending money or a car.

The survey revealed that today's adolescent faces many stressful situations. To believe that young people "have it much easier than we did when we were their age," is a real disservice to the teenagers.

Since no man, woman, boy or girl is an island, what is stress for one family member will become stress for everyone in the family. It is my hope that when the going gets rough for young people and their parents, the entire family will reach out for help before misunderstanding and negative feelings toward one another get out of hand. A little bit of help can make a world of difference.

RAISING CHILDREN BY THE BOOKS

My mother taught me to read at age 3 by placing me in bed with her as she read to me from comic books. Thus, she inculcated in me a thirst for reading that has not been quenched, even to this day. My wife and I intentionally endeavored to raise our son and daughter to be readers, believing that a child who masters reading can master almost any subject. Here are a few simple techniques that will assist any parent in "raising children by the books."

Let Your Children See You Read

Children imitate their parents. They talk like their parents, walk like their parents, play "mommy and daddy," "mowing the lawn," and "doing the dishes" in imitation of their parents. If your youngsters see you curled up in your favorite chair with an absorbing book, laughing with Maya Angelou, in deep thought with James Baldwin, pondering with C. S. Lewis and crying with Madeline L'Engle, they will probably be attracted to the benefits of reading.

Conversely, however, if you're accustomed to evenings of "Designing Women" instead of Little Women, the appeals of a good book might not be so obvious to your son or daughter.

Read to Your Children

Amazingly, this technique smacks of common sense. However, it's amazing how few parents today read to their children, or inexplicably discontinue the practice as their children get older.

I returned to read Robert Louis Stevenson's Treasure Island a few years ago. As I re-read that which was a part of my high school and college studies, it suddenly dawned on me why the book was so popular. It was a children's classic because it was a favorite book for parents to read to their children. Books by Mark Twain are among my favorites. Kenneth Grahame's <u>The Wind in the Willows</u>, C.S. Lewis' series <u>The Chronicles of Narnia</u>, A. A. Milne's <u>Winnie the Pooh</u> and Pearl Buck's <u>The Story Bible</u> will provide hours of reading enjoyment for child and parent.

Let Your Children Occasionally Read to You

As my children's reading skills developed, they began to enjoy books that allowed them to follow along as I read aloud. Soon, I discovered that I could enjoy our times of togetherness much more by allowing them to take turns reading to me from books written at their reading level. As a father I would have an overwhelming gush of pride and enjoyment as I followed the words on the pages as my daughter and son read to me. I would study their faces as they read to me. Now I am getting that same rush as my two granddaughters read to me. When they come to my home, they rush to my library and set me down in my reading chair and joyfully read to me, taking turns.

Take Children to the Library—Often

During my children's growing up years, the public library, or the college library, would be an anticipated "field trip."

Children being among so many children's books are enormously stimulated and children will take pride in possessing their own library card. Sometimes my children would sit down in the library and begin reading a book. More often they would "check-out" their selections of choice and begin reading as we drove back home.

Subscribe to Magazines and Book Clubs

Our family friends would often express amazement at the number of subscriptions and book club memberships we maintain—even today.

With our children they were included in the book clubs and sub-scriptions. Now they follow that same pattern with their children.

Sure, budgets for book purchases may be limited, however even when books cannot be purchased, the book club bulletins represent "good reading." They help children to make better choices when they go to the neighborhood library.

Make Reading a Privilege

Children always seek to have later bedtimes. Why not extend the bedtimes by allowing the last 30 minutes as "reading time." You will be surprised at the result of extending the curfew by providing extra time reading in bed.

Place interesting books throughout the home. Give each child a small bookcase of his or her own. Reserve several high-quality books each year for long motor trips, being sure to put the books in the backpack that your child will certainly pack and take on the trip.

Make sure books are also liberally included in birthday and holi-day celebrations, developing in your children a strong appreciation for the smell and feel of a new book. I have long practiced making books my favorite gift to others—even to this day.

Raising a child by the books can widen horizons, stimulate imagination, lessen the influence of television, encourage the dis-covery of new interests, strengthen family togetherness and provide a storehouse of fond memories for parent and child.

Of course, that's not all there is to being a parent. But it makes an effective beginning.

NO CASUALTIES AT CHRISTMAS

How to Prevent Children From Succumbing to Greediness During the Christmas Season

Christmas is a celebration of giving and receiving. Unfortunately, parents usually concentrate on giving while their children focus on receiving.

As holiday spending gains momentum, television commercials bombard children with displays of the most up-to-date toys. These glittering performances can transform mild mannered, generous children into greedy monsters.

How can parents prevent children from becoming casualties of Christmastime greediness? Here are a few suggestions to help your child become as enthralled with giving as he is with receiving.

Use the Name of Santa Claus Less

Santa often seems more synonymous with Christmas than Christ. No wonder children focus more on getting from Santa than on giving, as our Lord's birth represents.

When your child begins a "Santa" sentence, try to reroute the thought process. Ask the child to think of a good gift for Santa to bring someone else—a neighbor, relative or friend. Remind your child that thinking about others and their needs is important, because that was what Jesus did when He came down to earth.

Keep the list short. Have your child begin a Christmas "wish list." Each time he mentions a new toy, instruct him/her to add it to his list. A few days before you begin your shopping, tell your child the list must be narrowed down. This allows your child to begin assessing his needs as opposed to his wants. Now you are providing valuable lessons on making choices.

Allow Your Child to Give

Many children do not feel they are a real part of Christmas giving. When parents purchase gifts for themselves from their child, the child will have difficulty understanding that the gift is really from him.

To help your child experience the giving spirit, let him help choose the gifts he will give to relatives, friends, or teachers. Even giving your child two items from which to choose provides the child with a sense of participation. Allowing your child to handle the money in the transaction is a helpful teaching lesson.

Compose a Prayer List

Help your child prepare a list of the needs of others. Describe a situation to the child, such as a friend who needs a job or an elderly neighbor who has been ill. Ask your child's advice as to how to pray for these needs. Should you pray that God helps the friend find a job and that He helps the elderly neighbor feel better?

As your child makes suggestions, add them to the list. Schedule a special time for reading the child's prayer list. Perhaps Christmas Eve would be a good time for the entire family to pray for those people and their needs.

With a little encouragement, your child will begin to be aware of the needs of others. The best thing about the child's prayer list is that the child can continue to use it long after the holiday season is over. After all, the best way for any of us to beat the "I want" syndrome is to focus on others, whatever the season.

This Christmas, take a few extra minutes to help your child learn that true Christmas joy is found in giving, not getting!

TWELVE RULES
FOR RAISING CHILDREN

RULE #1   - Remember that a child is a gift from God, the richest of all blessing. Do not attempt to mold the child in the image of yourself, your father, your brother, or your neighbor. Each child is an individual and should be permitted to be himself.

RULE #2   - Don't crush your child's spirit when he fails. And never compare your child with others who may outshine.

RULE #3   - Remember that anger and hostility are natural emotions. Help your child to find socially acceptable outlets for these normal feelings or they may be turned inward and erupt in the form of physical or mental illness.

RULE #4   - Discipline your child with firmness and reason. Don't let YOUR anger throw you off balance. If the child knows you are fair, you will not lose respect or love. And make sure the punishment fits the crime. Even the youngest child has a keen sense of justice.

RULE #5   - Remember that each child needs two parents. Present a unified front. Never join with your child against your mate. This can create emotional conflicts in your child (as in yourself). It can also create feelings of guilt, confusion and insecurity.

RULE #6   - Do not hand your child everything that the heart desires. Permit the child to know the thrill of earning and the joy of achieving. Instill in your child the greatest of all satisfactions, the pleasure that comes with personal accomplishment.

RULE #7 - Do not set yourself up as the epitome of perfection. This is a difficult role to play 24 hours a day. You will find it easier to communicate if it is known that Mom and Dad can make mistakes too.

RULE #8 - Don't make threats in anger or impossible promises when you are in a generous mood. Threaten or promise only that which you can live up to. A parent's word means everything to a child. Any son or daughter who has lost faith in their parents has difficulty believing in anything.

RULE #9 - Do not smother your child with superficial manifestations of "love." Pure and healthy love expresses itself in day-in, day-out training, which breeds self-confidence and independence.

RULE #10 - Teach your child that there is dignity in hard work, whether it is performed with callused hands that shovel coal or skilled fingers that manipulate surgical instruments. Let the child know that a useful life is a blessed one and that a life of ease and pleasure-seeking is empty and meaningless.

RULE #11 - Do not try to protect your child against every small blow or disappointment. Adversity strengthens character and makes us compassionate. Trouble is the great equalizer. Let the child learn that valuable lesson.

RULE #12 - Teach your child to love God and to love his fellow men. Don't send your child to a place of worship; take him there. Children learn from example. Telling is not teaching. Remember that a deep and abiding faith in God can be the child's strength and his light when all else fails.[2]

---

2 Co-authors note: adapted from two columns of Ann Landers that appeared in the Dallas Morning News.

DISCIPLINE, A GIFT OF LOVE

Of the many hazards involved with parenting, one of the worst seems to be how to discipline our children. In fact, most of what parents do for their children involves discipline in one form or another.

However, we must not confuse discipline with punishment, for they are two different things. Discipline is the continual, daily process of helping a child, a young person, gain self-control. No one is born with self-discipline. As parents administer love and discipline to children, children learn to control themselves.

Disciplining a child, or a young person, is one of the most caring things a parent can do for your offspring and can be one of the greatest satisfactions of parenthood.

Discipline involves comfort, care, nurture and the passing on of traditions and values unique to one's family. It includes reward and praise for activities well done. And it includes providing—by example—rules, limitations and positive qualities to children.

Discipline is a learning process within a relationship. By helping children learn to be self-disciplined, we also help them become independent. We are teaching them how to be, in turn, loving parents to their children.

The word discipline is based on the word "disciple." The disciple of a spiritual leader is one who leans on the leader's teachings. We think of one who is intimately involved with the leader because he or she loves that person. This principle applies directly to parenting.

Disciplining a child is based on a series of rules. Rules can also be understood as setting limits. Everyone needs to observe limits throughout life. Our parents now gave many of the limits we place on ourselves to us. We tested those limits, especially during the teen and young adult years, but those we found valuable became part of our growing self-discipline.

Children, when young, need many limits. Some are set for their health and safety, others to help them move comfortably among their peers. Happy and healthy family life depends on set limits. Such limits keep family life moving on schedules that reflect the needs of various family members. Other family limits serve to protect privacy and property.

The reassurance of having limits is important for the healthy emotional growth of children. Children and teens feel safer when they know what the rules are. They feel safer when people they love have told them the rules or limits.

It is important that children be permitted to "feel their feelings." But they need limits set on the expression of those feelings. Not only can the environment <u>outside</u> the home be frightening, but also the world <u>inside</u>, the world of feelings, can be scary when one is not sure he or she can handle those feelings alone.

Good rules or limits are practical, within the child's capability, consistent, express loving concern and serve reasonable purposes.

Limit setting should always be done within a loving and nurturing atmosphere, for love is the root of all good discipline. And love is the root of helping a child learn self-discipline.

But love, and the fear of losing love, may also be at the root of many parent's discomfort when it comes to setting and maintaining limits. The desire to be loved is a powerful motivation for all of us. Parents need to find the security within themselves to accept the reality that they and their children won't always like each other's actions, and that there will be times when parents and children won't be "friends." There will be times of real anger within the family.

Parents also need to keep in mind that, even in moments of conflict, they and their children can still love each other. We may love our children but not be pleased with their actions. And sometimes a child may not like the actions of parents, but will still love them.

As parents continue to consistently demonstrate love for their children, they are helping them become all they can be. For children can develop well only if they are capable of making good choices and observing necessary limits through self-control.

WHEN RULES ARE BROKEN

In the previous essay the subject of discipline was addressed. Attention was directed to the difference between discipline and punishment, and the need for rules, boundaries and limits. This essay is designed to explore punishment specifically.

What happens when rules are broken? For parents who stress limit setting rather than punishment, reward is generally more important than a spanking. They believe that the continual display of appreciation for a child's observance of limits matters most.

But in every family a little rain must fall sometimes. There will be occasions when it will be necessary to punish the child. But who punishes the child? In what way? To what extent?

The appropriateness of a punishment depends on the unique personality and experiences of each parent and each child, and even more importantly on the quality of the relationship between parent and child.

The way we choose to punish our children is often based on the way we were punished as children. Characteristics of parenting seem to be transferred from one generation to the next.

The expression of punishment also has a lot to do with cultural traditions and values. And what deserves to be punished and what can be left unpunished is determined by these cultural considerations.

There is a big difference between power punishment and loving punishment. Power punishment tends to be a reaction to something perceived as a personal challenge or a response to something that threatens a parent's sense of security as a parent.

Power punishments are usually associated with angry statements such as: "You never listen to what I say! This will teach you who's boss! This is my house and as long as you live in it, you abide by my rules!" Power punishments typically include physical punishments such as spanking.

In contrast, loving punishments tend to be firm reminders to the child of limits that, for health, safety or practical reasons, he or she must observe. I must admit that it was a learning experience for me, as a grandfather, to comprehend the utilization of "time out" as a form of loving punishment displayed by my daughter and son as they lovingly punish the only-child daughter in each of their families.

So a parent might remind a child, "You know you're not supposed to leave the yard because you might get hurt in the street. Now you'll have to stay indoors, where I can keep an eye on you." Or a parent might say, "I can understand that you're angry, but no one wants to hear all that noise. You can go to your room until you find a quieter way of showing that you're mad."

Loving punishments are likely to include restrictions on activity, the curtailing of something pleasurable or the revoking of privileges. For instance, in loving punishment a parent may take away video games or television for a few days.

Loving punishments suggest consistency. Both parents must agree on these punishments. One cannot change the other's disciplinary action, no matter how much he or she disagrees with the punishment chosen.

In addition, loving punishment is generally something both parents can live with. If one parent decides that a child is to be grounded for three days, both parents must follow through for three days. To give in to the child's coaxing, to change the punishment to one day is not good for the child or the parents.

It's a rare parent, though, who hasn't lost his or her temper at some time and reacted verbally or physically with a power punishment. The one occasion when I can recall having resorted to power punishment with my son was when I learned that he and his next door buddy decided to play hooky from school and just "hang out" one day. With that action being a clear violation of the values and rules that had been instilled, power punishment followed in his room when I came home from the university that evening.

However, I used that time as a positive learning experience for my son and me. There was never a occasion subsequently when there was a need for power punishment. Children at all ages can learn a great deal when, after the heat of the moment has passed, the parent apologizes (which I did) for having to resort to such drastic measures with the son that I love so deeply.

Having apologized—which is often hard for adults but necessary as a learning process for all concerned—you can then find a loving punishment that will help your child observe in the future the necessary limits you have set.

A constructive punishment has two important characteristics:

- It should follow closely after the behavioral problem; it should be within the scope of the child's understanding, for example, making the punishment fit the deed.
- There should be a firm distinction between the behavior and the child. Your children need to realize that you are upset with their behavior but that you still love them as individuals.

RESPECT IS A TWO-WAY STREET

Having addressed discipline and punishment in the two previous essays, we want to now draw attention to the imperative of respect.

Child psychologists recognize that children are born with a natural curiosity, which leads them to challenge facts and authority. Rather than assuming that this curiosity is rude and disrespectful, parents should nurture it. For the child who questions grows up to be independent and able to make intelligent choices.

Many parents prefer—and demand—complete obedience and a non-questioning attitude. They perceive that as respect.

But child therapists understand that children who are blindly obedient and ask few questions of parental authority are more likely to succumb to peer pressure. They are more likely to follow friends or classmates in experimentation with marijuana, alcohol, drugs and other self-destructive activities.

Children and adolescents can often be momentarily rude in the way they speak to their parents, but this does not mean that they are being disrespectful of parental authority. If an adolescent shouts at his father in a fit of anger, he may be expressing temporary frustration, possibly not even meant for his parents.

True disrespect is a much more consistent rejection of rules, and is an expression of a great deal of underlying anger, not merely momentary frustration.

Hostile, anti-social behavior is a signal that a child wants, and needs, more discipline of a consistent nature from both parents. When parents are consistent in their rule setting and decision-making, a child is more apt to stay comfortable within the limits that have been set. That child may be more respectful of parents' rights and feelings, as well as others.

All children need to feel that their feelings, actions and questions are meaningful to parents who love them. In fact, listening to their questions and making useful comments about them displays love and admiration by parents for their children. Without such rewards, youngsters can lose their motivation to please authority figures.

Giving children praise and attention conveys parents' interest in them. This interest serves to promote youngster's sense of self-esteem and responsibility.

Therefore, parents should encourage children's questions and should answer them as clearly and honestly as possible. In this way the experience becomes a growth-producing endeavor for both.

Adolescents who question life will not blindly follow peers in self-destructive activities. A challenging child who questions can be a real delight to his or her parents, not a disrespectful, hostile, or anti-social person with little self-worth.

When parents nurture and cherish a child's questioning and independent nature, the youngster develops a greater capacity to cope with life's hurdles and rewards later on. And when a child is given the respect and praise he or she deserves, he or she will give the same respect and praise to parents.

Of course, praise must be justified. Simply praising youngsters to make them feel better—when they have not earned praise—is neither honest nor sincere. This can weaken the meaning of praise.

But honest praise and reward given to a child by attentive, listening parents promotes a positive parent-child relationship. Respect is a two-way street for parents and children.

SELF-ESTEEM IS BASIC

Having addressed discipline, punishment and respect in the three previous essays, attention is now directed to self-esteem. Parents who respect their children wish them success in life. And basic to children's success in whatever they do is their sense-of-self, who they are as individuals.

If children are encouraged by their parents to develop a sense of responsibility, they will gain the assurance they need. And when children gain a high sense of self-worth, their chances of attaining their goals in life are greatly increased.

On the other hand, if children are discouraged by parents who put them down, their self-worth will be damaged and they will not accomplish their goals.

Why is self-esteem so important and how can parents assess children's feelings about themselves? One's sense of self-esteem is made up of thoughts, feelings and ideas a person has about himself. It is the overall acceptance and respect for himself that counts.

In one way or another, feelings people have about themselves dictate how they will do in life. The type of friends children choose, the type of people they marry, their creativity, achievements and basic personality are all affected to some degree by their perception of who they are.

A strong self-esteem is not only the foundation of strong personality development, but also helps chart the child's life-course for happiness and success.

Consequently, the building of a strong self-image in children constitutes one of the greatest challenges of parenthood. But often parents are ill equipped to help create a positive self-image because of their own negative self-image.

Parents cannot teach their youngsters what they have not learned themselves. So raising a child is a second chance for parents to gain for themselves the self-esteem they lack.

We are not suggesting that parents should gain their sense of who they are by living vicariously through the deeds—or misdeeds—of their offspring. We are suggesting that parents can grow in their self-esteem along with their youngsters. By sharing a growing experience, each can develop a more positive sense of who they are as a person.

No one is born with high or low feelings about himself or herself. Self-esteem is learned from our interaction with important people in our lives, such as parents, grandparents, uncles and aunts. If we don't gain self-esteem from a positive interaction with one family member, we may gain it from another.

But, of course, the most important people in our lives as children are our parents. When this shared experience is with them, it becomes an even more potent growth-producing relationship.

The way we respect or disrespect ourselves begins from birth, when we relate to our parents and they relate to us. Experiences in the early years of life form the basic foundation of our feelings toward ourselves. However, these feelings are constantly being revised throughout our lives as the result of each additional experience we have.

It is never too late to develop better self-worth, either in ourselves or in those around us. Respect shown by parents to their children can only increase the youngster's self-esteem. Disrespect shown by parents to their children can only decrease the youngster's self-esteem.

The old adage, "Do unto others as you would have them do unto you," is still true. If parents start early to show respect to their children, their children will show respect and gain self-esteem.

A WORD OF ADVICE

You may recall Wilson, the faceless neighbor on the popular television show "Home Improvement," who always seems to have the right bit of advice to his friend Tim. Wilson talks with Tim while puttering around in his backyard. The fence always prevents the view of Wilson's face but it doesn't stop his words of wisdom from reaching Tim's ears.

The nuggets that he provides include advice on parenting, how to get along with others in the workplace and how Tim can better romance his wife. Wilson is not the nosy neighbor type, he only offers advice when requested.

In real life there aren't many Wilson's living next door to us. There are very few of us in this day and age that literally turn to our neighbor for advice. In far too many cases we only know our neighbor by name. Yet the sources of helpful pointers are plentiful and readily available to any would-be seeker.

Calls to psychic hotlines are very popular and very expensive. Advice columns abound in local newspapers and magazines, and are read religiously by millions every day. Radio call-in shows offer a host of advice selections. On any given day listeners can get professional counsel on almost any conceivable subject without ever leaving home. And it's all free!

When looking for advice it's helpful to get the information you need from a person who knows what they're talking about. If you have trouble with your car you don't go to your family physician for counsel. You go to a qualified mechanic who'll identify the problem and repair it.

King Solomon in the Bible penned a letter full of advice to his sons and to any of us who have ears to listen. The key verses are in Proverbs 3:5-6: "Trust in the Lord with all your heart and do not lean on your own understanding. In all your ways acknowledge Him, and He will make your paths straight."

Jesus too gave His listeners very practical and helpful advice in the famous Sermon on the Mount. In this discourse one can find tips on issues like how to relate to enemies, how to pray and how to overcome anxiety. In all the situations that confront us in life, Jesus' words are helpful to remember: "But seek first His kingdom and His righteousness; and all these things shall be added to you" (Matthew 6:33).

Jesus Christ can bring hope to any troubled heart perplexed by the questions life brings. Seek Him while you still have the opportunity, because when you come right down to it, that's the best advice available!

SIMPLICITY ALA FORREST GUMP

We read somewhere these lines: "Life is like a box of chocolates, you never know what you are going to get until you bite into it." This has become a very popular line from the hit movie that hit the wide screen in 1994, <u>Forrest Gump</u>. Academy award winning actor Tom Hanks plays the lead, a good natured fellow with an IQ of 75.

Despite his lack of outstanding intelligence, Forrest Gump somehow manages to become an inspiration to Elvis; stars on Alabama's Crimson Tide football team; becomes a hero of the Vietnam War; meets three presidents; opens diplomatic doors with China via the ping pong paddle; and becomes extremely wealthy.

The success of the movie was due in part to a creative story and a talented actor bringing to life a character that all people love to root for. "I don't think there's really any big message that comes out of this," Hanks said in an interview, "other than as a nation, we've been through a lot. After all of Forrest's triumphs and tragedies, what's the most important thing to him at the end of the day? <u>It's to let his kid know that he loves him</u>."

The childlike character of Forrest Gump calls to mind the power of simplicity. Only certain things in life really matter, like enjoying each day as it comes, pursuing your dreams and hugging your children. It seems that children possess many of the essential attributes that adults long for.

Although Forrest Gump was not intelligent, he was blessed with great speed. When he was told to run, he ran. He didn't question, or plan, or fret, or think it over. He accepted the command and blessings came his way. In turn, he was a blessing to others.

The message of the gospel is simple. Believe and receive. Jesus says "Come unto me and I will give you rest." Accepting the call from Christ is a challenge to some. For others it sounds too silly or simplistic. But becoming childlike in your faith is essential to eternal life. Receive the blessing of God in your life today by entering into a personal relationship with Jesus Christ.

ALTERNATIVES TO SCREAMING

Food For Thought For Mothers

Mothers have you ever felt like screaming? We are confident that you have had that experience. Although you feel like it, you know that your children can't stand you screaming. Yet, many continue to scream. What is it that drives mothers to lose control?

Although the "screaming habit" breeds guilt in mothers, it can be difficult to break. Why? Because many mothers are comfortable with the results of screaming. It usually guarantees a measure of success. The screaming mom will tolerate the guilt that follows the screaming episode. Changing behavior always involves substantial risk. In the case of screaming, mothers are apprehensive to exchange a familiar habit (which brings predictable results) for the unknown benefits of quiet control.

However, there are alternatives to screaming that can give such success to the mother that her confidence level will soar. Strong, controlled and confident mothers are capable of raising confident and controlled children. True strength is expressed through gentleness and self-control.

That mother who is cool and collected, who is master of her countenance, her voice, her actions and her gestures, will be the mother who is in control of her children, and who is greatly beloved by them.

If the truth be told, mothers set the tone of the home. When the mother is in control, the children are much easier to keep under control. But when the mother is upset, the children are usually "off the wall." Children are quite sensitive; they respond dramatically to the emotional pulse of the mother.

The following are some positive ways to gain control based on my own experience and my research.

- Plan ahead—a controlled mother is organized.
- Be flexible—a controlled mother is flexible for circumstances can dictate mid-course changes.
- Have a sense of humor—the mother who can laugh at herself, with her children and at the impossible situations of life is far ahead on the road to personal control.
- Don't lose your balance—the controlled mother strives to keep balance in her life. You have to balance the multitude of commitments that you have. Achieving balance can change your attitude toward your children.
- Give yourself permission to change. Our habits are formed throughout life by the people and situations we encounter.
- Make a firm decision to change—it takes a definite decision and commitment to change from being a "screamer."
- Consider what upsets you so much—knowing how you feel and why you feel that way will enable you to make a pivotal decision.
- Find some help—the one sure source is God, who is always on call. Don't forget to contact Him for the patience and wisdom you will need.[3]

---

3   Abstracted from When You Feel Like Screaming (1988) by Pat Holt and Grace Ketterman. Used by permission.

THE GENIE IS US

Children are the same everywhere, and Walt Disney's animated film Aladdin is certainly a film for children. You perhaps will also remember the classic rags-to-riches tale from Arabian Nights.

Aladdin is a resourceful youth who dreams of escaping his street-life existence and marrying the Sultan's beautiful daughter, Princess Jasmine. He is recruited by the Sultan's scheming advisor, Jafar to retrieve a magic lamp from deep within the Cave of Wonders. It can only be rescued by someone "whose rags hide a heart that is pure."

With the aid of his pal the genie, his pet monkey Abu and a magic carpet, Aladdin sets out to prove himself worthy of the princess by saving the kingdom from Jafar's evil plot.

It's the stuff of dreams. Who has never dreamt of being granted three wishes? Even one wish would be wonderful, but surely shouldn't be wasted on anything less than world peace or an end to hunger. With three, however, you might feel entitled to use one for yourself.

So what would you wish for? Health, wealth, happiness, long life, absolute freedom?

One of Aladdin's two Oscars was for best original song, "A Whole New World." While it is a beautiful romantic ballad, it offers little practical help to anyone searching for the source of happiness.

True happiness is found not in the selfish acquisition of wealth, or the pursuit of fame or power, but in helping others. It's infinitely more rewarding to give than to receive.

Over the years millions of Jesus' followers have discovered that obeying the command in John 15:12—"my commandment is this, love one another," is critical. Obeying that command brings such peace and happiness that it makes the treasures of Aladdin's cave insignificant.

Like the Cave of Wonders, though, these treasures are only fully found by those "whose rags hide a heart that is pure."

GETTING PAST THE FIRST STEP

It's like riding a bike, as the old saying goes. Once you've learned how to do it, you never forget.

That development stage was reached with me and my two children, particularly my daughter. It was also reached by my children with their children (who happen to be daughters also). Our daughter reached the point where she wanted to move from the training wheels to one without the wheels.

When I made the plunge and brought the bicycle home there were some immediate changes. The old bike stood upright on its own. It did not wobble. The new five-gear, drop-handlebar model suddenly looked more like a nightmare than a dream machine.

A new world beckoned. A world of excitement, enjoyment and freedom. But this world of adventure could not be entered without pain.

During a session of biking that contained more spills than thrills, one thing was clear. While my daughter could ride without help or hindrance from dad once she got started, the hardest step to take was the first step. It was the initial push of the pedal that was proving so difficult. This ride of passage would have to wait for another day.

To be fair, it's not as easy as it looks. There's a lot to contend with. There's the weight of the bike, the coordination of the body, the excitement of success, the fear of getting hurt, the dread of falling. After all, there is nothing so easy as falling off a bike.

To many people, living out the Christian faith appears just as daunting. Jesus offers us a world so new, so exciting, and so different that He describes it like being born all over again.

Jesus offers us freedom. He promises a journey with a purpose. His company through life's up and downs, and His comfort when we fall. But somehow that first step of faith is so hard to take.

We want to hold onto what we know and hand ourselves over to God at the same time. We're attracted by forgiveness, but held back by fear. We're afraid of missing out, yet afraid of messing up. We are going nowhere fast. We are in turmoil.

But we don't have to struggle alone. "Don't be afraid," God assures us, "for I am with you." In Him we have a heavenly Father who holds us, guides us and encourages us to leave our fears and launch out in tandem with Him. After that first step, you'll be on your way.

Is this not helpful advice for parents, children and young adults? I think so.

FOREVER FRIENDS

Two preschoolers celebrate life in a sandbox. Sunshine. Shovels and pails. And a friend. What more could you ask?

One of them may wonder why the other has a different skin tone; but it isn't important. A child may recognize that the friend attends a different church or no church at all, but that's not important, it doesn't matter.

What matters is the celebration of life—together. You see, friendship holds a magical quality. What starts in the sandbox can continue through life.

In school, best friends find each other. A teacher may follow a student's progress long after the year's final report card. At summer camp, special bonds are forged; worker to worker, camper to counselor, and children to leader.

At home, a girl matures into womanhood and discovers her mother is a friend, not a foe, and not just a parent.

Two strangers sit on a park bench, or at the bus stop. They chat, exchange phone numbers, go out for coffee. A friendship is born.

Sometimes it requires extra effort when the male meets the female. There may be several disastrous dates before the magic of romance begins. There may be differences of opinion, but as two become special to each other, the differences are no longer important. However it happens, friendship is crucial to our lives. Love brings a measure of joy and satisfaction to our lives. Loneliness is an enemy.

The Bible tells us about a special friendship forged between Jesus Christ and His disciples. They entered a new world when they encountered Him; their lives changed forever.

Jesus no longer walks the earth in physical form, but His presence is here. And his friendship is real. He offers it to anyone who yearns to be loved and accepted unconditionally.

He's reaching out to you now, promising to end your loneliness, to fill your life with joy. He will always be there when you need Him; He will always listen when you speak. He loves you.

You may be long past the sandbox, but you're never too old to celebrate life. Why not celebrate it with the greatest Friend of all?

As parents, we have a responsibility to inculcate true friendship in the lives of our children. As adults there is the imperative of practicing being a friend to others.

PART IV

GUIDANCE FOR LIFE'S JOURNEY

YESTERDAY ONCE MORE

Imagine waking up every morning at exactly the same time, with the same song playing on the radio, and discovering that every day is literally the same as the day before.

That was the scenario for the 1993 movie, <u>Ground-hog Day</u>, in which comedian Bill Murray plays self-centered TV weatherman Phil Connors, who is sent by his Pittsburgh station to report the annual Groundhog Day ceremonies in Punxsutawney, Pennsylvania.

Connors finds himself snowed in by a blizzard and becomes trapped in the town, not just for an extra night, but forever.

Caught in a time-warp, he is condemned to live that February day over and over and over again, beginning with the bedside radio waking him up at six o'clock each morning with "I've Got You, Babe," by Sonny and Cher.

Director Harold Ramis said, "The real fun of this film is to imagine what you would do if you were stuck in the same day for eternity. Phil runs the gamut from confusion and misery to total hedonism. He's liberated from any consequences for his actions, and it's a lot of fun to see him explore what that would really mean in one's life."

The weatherman soon realizes that if there is no tomorrow, if acts have no consequences, you can do whatever you like—drive with reckless abandon, over-eat, upset everyone by your rudeness—then start the same day afresh the next morning.

At first, Phil relishes the situation and exploits the possibilities. Eventually though, he realizes he is trapped.

The comedy lies in the ideas of the film, rather than the action. The viewer is encouraged to think while he laughs—which is always a good thing.

Years ago, it was the sermon in church on Sunday that challenged people's moral standards. Nowadays, for many people, it seems the cinema or TV has taken over. Films like <u>Groundhog Day</u> pose ethical questions that beg for answers.

But can a movie provide answers as well as questions? Ultimately, the responsibility is on us to find the right answers. Happily, God has provided the help we need. All the right answers are found in His Word and the story of His Son, Jesus, who is "the way, the truth and the life" (John 14:6).

WHAT IS A FAMILY?

A family is a blessing,
It means so many things.
Words could never really tell
The joy a family brings.

A family is mutual love,
The love of a dad and mother,
Showing children how to love
And care for one another.

A family is heartfelt pride,
The feeling deep and strong,
That makes us glad to play a part.
And know that we belong.

A family is always home,
A place where we can share
Our joys and sorrows, hopes and dreams.
For happiness lives there.

A family is a bond of faith
That even time can't sever,
A gift to last throughout our lives –
A family is forever.

Author unknown
Copied from SHARE magazine with permission

TRUE LOVE WAITS

The International Year of the Family 1994 Theme

I served as a member of the Advisory Board to the Salvation Army of Dallas for nearly two decades. I recall that in 1994, working in conjunction with the Southern Baptist Sunday School Board, a major initiative was launched as a part of the International Year of the Family.

Recognizing the threat of AIDS and other sexually transmitted diseases, a campaign called "True Love Waits" was conducted by churches nationwide.

Based on the biblical mandate of marriage before sex, the "True Love Waits" program encouraged youth to sign commitment cards promising to remain sexually pure from that moment on.

Campaign Purpose

- To challenge families to address within the home biblical standards of sexual behavior.
- To communicate to teenagers the spiritual, emotional and physical value of remaining sexually pure until marriage.
- To provide churches with a way of supporting parents and teenagers as they express their commitment to sexual purity.
- To communicate to the world a preferred alternative to the "safe sex" message.

Campaign Theme

- True love for God.
- True love for your current date.
- True love for your future mate.
- True love for your future child.
- True love for yourself.

Guidelines for a Family Devotional Plan

- Center your family devotional time around God's plan for marriage and love.
- Ask: What would make this dream of lifelong love come true?
- Explain that one of the best ways to express these love qualities is through waiting until marriage for sex.
- Ask: What does it mean to be "sexually pure" before marriage.
- Read 1 Thessalonians 4:3-8 and 1 Corinthians 13:4-13 for a definition.
- Invite your teen to commit to abstain from sex before marriage and to commit to one-flesh purity after marriage.
- Pray together, thanking God for the gift of sexuality and the power to keep this commitment to live sexually pure lives.
- Hug or otherwise express affection for your teenager.
- Agree that making a commitment to sexual abstinence is easier than keeping the commitment.
- Pray for each other.
- Talk openly about each other's sexual pressures and offer support in resisting them.
- Encourage friendships with others who are waiting.
- Pray for a good spouse-to-be.
- Show confidence in your teenager.
- Give lots of love at home so away-from-home love won't be as craved.
- Together set limits for dating.

- Recognize and resist lies and false images.
- Assure each other that God will give you power.
- Choose one or more Bible verses to post in your home as a reminder to live sexually pure and loving lives.

Although this campaign was launched over a decade ago, when one surveys the current landscape, the need is as urgent now as it was then.

CLASSIC TALE UNLOCKS A SECRET

My wife and I have been privileged to make two visits to the United Kingdom, most recently to Oxford University. On each of our visits we were impressed with the architecture of the English homes.

A forbidding Gothic house on the windswept moors of England, a family with a dark secret and a beautiful hidden garden in which love and friendship can flower and troubles of the mind and body can be healed. That's the world in which Frances Hodgson Burnett set her classic children's novel, The Secret Garden, which was released as a feature film.

The Secret Garden tells how the lives and personalities of three lonely children are changed forever when they meet and forge friendships in a locked secret garden that becomes their special refuge.

It is a story about Mary Lennox, a little girl who lives in India. After a tragic earthquake in which her parents are killed, Mary is sent to England to live in her uncle's house, Mistlethwaite Manor.

There she meets her cousin, Colin, who is constantly told how ill he is. She also discovers a long-neglected garden, kept locked since Colin's mother died in childbirth.

Together with stable-boy Dicken, Mary frees Colin from his fear of fresh air, and in the secret garden Colin regains his health. There too, Mary discovers her own miracle.

Through the opening of the garden and Colin's transformation, Mary's uncle, Lord Craven, learns to laugh again, and Mary learns to cry—something she has been unable to do since the trauma she suffered in India.

"You did something I thought no one could do," her uncle tells her. "I won't shut it out again."

To many people, God is a mystery shut away behind locked doors. The benefits of knowing Him—joy, peace of mind, purpose in life—are perhaps recognized, but the step of unlocking the door to them is avoided through fear of the unknown.

The Apostle Paul, in his writing and preaching, tried to convey the means of knowing God. The secret, he explained, lies in Jesus.

"My purpose is . . . that they may have the full riches of complete understanding, in order that they may know the mystery of God, namely Christ, in whom are hidden all the treasures of wisdom and knowledge" (Col. 2:2-3).

For too many people, religious faith in general and Jesus Christ in particular are like a secret garden the existence of which they are ignorant, or which they fear to enter. Take a risk and discover the secret to the full life in Jesus Christ!

STAY-TOGETHER FAMILIES

As we penned this essay, we were struck by a major current topic in the media, the divorce rate in this country. An interesting facet of the news coverage is the data that show an alarming increase in the number of men and women who "live together" before they get married. Equally alarming was the fact that those who "lived together" had a higher divorce rate than those who followed the traditional and Biblical pattern for marriage. Those alarming facts served as the impetus for this little piece.

Each stage of family life, with its unlimited variations, requires patience, openness and love. It also requires wisdom and understanding—and a deep desire and commitment from those involved to make it work.

The Beginning Years

Babies, diapers, bottles, crying, sleeplessness, toddlers, potty-training, more babies. So wonderful and new at first.

But following that stage most people realize they no longer have the energy to go through it again. So much time is needed to care for those precious little lives.

It is a time, unfortunately, when husband and wife can drift apart. He can feel rejected or left out. She can be too busy to note. He can be too busy with trying to carve out a career to be fully aware of details on the "home front."

This is an extremely important time for establishing spiritual awareness within the framework of the family. Even the very youngest must sense that parents are working together to raise their children. It's a feeling of inner security for them.

As an added dimension for Christian families, children need to intuitively know that Jesus Christ is the center of their parents' lives and thus the center of their family life.

The School Years

In many cases, a young mother's first taste of freedom is when her children start school. Yet it is a time of adjustment. Children suddenly come home using strange words (often four-letter) they heard at school. Some act in a defiant manner in order to assert their individuality. This is a time when ground rules must be set in place. Family time is vital, interaction is crucial.

Family devotions can be a time when children feel free to ask questions, discuss concerns, and express their opinions. Children must know that as part of the family they're free to talk any part of their lives—physical, emotional, spiritual.

Adolescence

Adolescents are in a constant metamorphosis as they progress from childhood to adulthood. They are fluctuating between dependence and a desire for total independence. Secular society strives to lure teens away from what is right and good. All this causes confusion, tension, rebellion and anger.

During this time parents are reaching their middle years. For some, that is a crisis. They can no longer do all they once could. Hair begins to turn grey. Bodies take on a different shape. Often these changes cause tensions within the marriage.

A family that can stay together in terms of communication, openness and mutual respect can eventually pray together. The prayers may not be polished at first. But there can be an affirmation that prayer for one another is taking place. Teens need their privacy. A personal devotional time is extremely healthy and to be greatly encouraged. But they must be aware that parents also give priority to their devotional life.

Parents demand great respect from their teenagers. But they must also be willing to give respect. Teens need to see their parents' care and love for one another. Mutual understanding and patience is required from all members of the family. God will honor the love and concern we have for our adolescents. He will grant wisdom as families strive to show each other who Jesus Christ is and the important role He can play in their lives.

Family Unity

As stated at the beginning of this essay, the number of families today that stay together through thick and thin is rapidly decreasing. Many call it quits when the going gets tough. Yet God calls us to commitment and wholeness.

We are responsible for the fracturing, the brokenness, and the pain. As Christians we need to put the broken pieces back together.

It takes effort and courage. It also takes humility. All God asks is to be placed at the center of every relationship, every family. He must be the focus of all we do and say. Every stage of family life is unique. But with His help and guidance blended with our total commitment, all things are possible.

THE GIFT OF LIFE

A Salvation Army officer told the story of where in the small coastal town of Bodega Bay, California, family and church friends gathered in a country church to remember a boy whose tragic death gave life.

Seven-year-old Nicholas Green was shot by highway robbers while sleeping in the back seat of a car driven by his father. He was on vacation with his family in Italy. His sister, Eleanor, was also shot, yet she managed to survive.

Days later, Nicholas was declared brain dead. In an act of generosity that shocked an entire nation, his parents donated Nicholas' liver, kidneys, heart and pancreas. These were then transplanted to five seriously ill Italian children. This was unusual because Italy is known to have one of the world's lowest organ donor rates.

At Nicholas' memorial service, his father Reginald said, "He has already helped save the lives of other children and indirectly perhaps many more in the future. He could have lived to be 100 and done less."

Reginald Green says the easiest decision he and his wife made was to give their son's body parts to extend life to other. He adds, "He also has struck a spark of love in the hearts of millions of parents and children around the world. If this isn't immortality, it must surely come close." Nicholas' gift of life will not soon be forgotten by the people Italy.

There is a major message in this story; it is something to be remembered by each of us. Some 2,000 years ago when God extended His love to us through the life-gift of Jesus Christ, a standard for living was set.

The day before His crucifixion, Jesus illustrated the concept for His disciples: "He took bread, gave thanks and broke it, and gave it to them, saying, 'This is my body given for you' "(Luke 22:19).

Jesus gave His life that we might live. The parents of Nicholas gave his organs so that others might live. Both acts were unselfish. It was through the unselfish sacrifice of Jesus that we can receive eternal life. "For even the Son of Man did not come to be served, but to serve, and to give His life as a ransom for many" (Mark 10:45).

Nicholas' organs represented a transaction made to save other lives. Jesus has already made the supreme transaction—His life for yours. What will you do with the offering of eternal life today?

THE REWARDS OF MOTHERHOOD

Motherhood Brings Plenty of
Job Satisfaction

Following the passing of my mother and my son's grandmother to her eternal home with God in 2001, my youngest sister joined me in helping me finish a memoir to our mother in the form of a book titled—<u>Celebrating Motherhood: the Life, Lessons and Legacy of Mother Dear</u>. This short article represents further reflections on my beautiful mother and how she was a wonderful mother to nine children. Also it represents lessons that I gleaned as I was the oldest of her children and had to function as a surrogate "mother" to my siblings as I helped my "mother dear."

Motherhood is a job that has its own special rewards. First of all, you get a free fitness program. You get to run obstacle courses around toys. You get to do stretches across beds to retrieve that hidden book. And you get to do lots of shoulder twists to see around little heads in front of the bathroom mirror.

Motherhood lets you set your own hours. You work the 28-hour day or the 30-hour day. It's up to you.

You also get to meet new people—like the history teacher—who wants to know why your daughter wrote on the test she wasn't sure who Lewis and Clark were, but thought she had their music video.

You travel. You get to drive to soccer practice, T-ball practice, piano lessons, basketball games, dental appointments, parent-teacher meetings, the Little League . . . and that's just on Monday.

You get to become a detective to solve such mysteries as who left the glass of milk behind the sofa, and what did he or she plan to do with the tree growing out of it?

You gain valuable judicial experience as well, as you determine, through the testimony of witnesses, whose turn it is to do the dishes or take out the trash.

A free telephone answering service is provided for you. Never again will you have to run to answer the phone. As a matter of fact, never again will it be for you. This is certainly true in this day of multiple cell phones in every home.

You get free on-the-job medical training as well. You'll learn how to dress a wound, break a fever and mend a broken heart.

You also get a free accounting service. If you forget how many weeks you're behind on your child's allowance, or how much you borrowed from the piggy bank last month, they have it totaled to the last penny and will gladly send a monthly statement.

But that's not all. You also get priceless gifts—cards with their handprints drawn on them, a ceramic heart tray made in crafts class, a Christmas tree ornament with their picture on it, the precious school days pictures each year. You won't find gifts like these at the mall.

Motherhood also offers a terrific stress reduction program. It's called "hug therapy," and somehow children always seem to know how to provide it at just the right moment.

You get job security, too. After all, no matter how much growing up your children do, you'll always be their mom.

But more importantly, motherhood brings plenty of job satisfaction from knowing you've done the best you can to mold and give direction to those precious lives God has placed in your care.

My hope and prayer is that these expressions from a male "surrogate mom" will have utility for the mothers in this contemporary world that we live in.

The hope of my son is that these expressions will have utility in the lives of parents and men of his generation.

Dr. Wright L. Lassiter, Jr.—circa 1934.
Wright L. Lassiter, III—circa 1963

THE MANE POINT

The Lion King, the block-buster animated film by Disney that was introduced in 1995, follows the story of Prince Simba, an African lion cub, whose father Mufasa is ruler of the Pride lands. As a care-free cub, Simba can't wait for the day he'll become a king. But his wicked uncle Scar hopes the day will never dawn and so plots to take the throne himself by killing both Mufasa and Simba.

Scar accomplishes the first part of the diabolical plan and blames a heartbroken Simba for the death of Mufasa.

Frightened and guilt-ridden, Simba flees into exile. But the past catches up to him and eventually he is called to return to the Pride lands. Scar's reign is causing great suffering and Simba is compelled to take his rightful place as king and thus save the pride (pack of lions).

Simba hears the voice of his father calling him to take his place in the circle of life. It's make-your-mind-up-time. Will he take on the job his father prepared him for? Or will he just take it easy? Feeling responsible is one thing; taking responsibility quite another.

This family film tells a familiar story. The Bible tells us Jesus was born to fulfill the plan of His Father by rescuing those who were in trouble. Jesus described the plan in these terms: "The Son of Man came to seek and to save what was lost" (Luke 19:10).

There were several times, though, when Jesus had to check with His Father to seek that He was on the right track. The most notable time was on the eve of His crucifixion when He asked God, "Take this cup from me. Yet not what I will, but what You will" (Mark 14:36).

Within hours of confirming God's plan for His life, Jesus was dead. Within days, God had brought Him back to life—as planned—

so that, in the words of Jesus, "whoever believes . . . shall not perish but have eternal life" (John 3:16).

As the story of Simba reminds us, taking responsibility is never easy. But as the life, death and resurrection of Jesus show, the rewards of obedience are worth more than even a lion king's ransom. You can claim your eternal inheritance by trusting Jesus.

The central lesson in this little essay is the imperative of taking responsibility.

A MAZING LIFE

The life we live is anything but simple and the future totally unpredictable. Day after day, a myriad of things seem to contradict what is known or accepted as truth. Existence itself becomes onerous and projecting goals appears useless. For many, life is a labyrinth. It is easy to get lost in its intricate windings—and to see no way out.

Deep in the labyrinth are young families, an increasing number of them headed by single parents. Each step taken takes them forward or backward, sometimes sideways. The pace at which they move is mind-boggling with inescapable pressures in the home and at work. Like labyrinth passages, one responsibility leads to another and though some light glimmers at the end of the maze, all energy is sapped.

Mid-life brings its own difficulties. Some people, hoping to escape from what they believe is a stagnant marriage, fall victim to the "greener grass" syndrome. The "empty nest" as children leave home diminishes the sense of being needed. At work, downsizing can result in loss of self-worth.

While some elderly persons find fulfillment in their golden years, others sadly feel abandoned and are achingly lonely. As their children deal with their own labyrinths, parents take second, even third place.

Strength of mind and heart is needed to cope with this mysterious, difficult life. How do we make the journey with a sense of determination and joy? Is there really any hope?

The answers are found in a personal intimate relationship with Christ, for hope and strength can only be found in Him.

Thomas, a disciple of Christ, often felt lost in the maze of life. "How can we know the way?" he asked. Jesus' encouraging answer is true for every believer today: "I am the Way, the Truth and the

Life" (John 14:6). For Thomas, as for everyone weaving their way through life's labyrinth, Jesus is the only Way to inner peace and joy.

May this lesson and the teaching principle be helpful to all.

NINE AFFORDABLE GIFTS THAT TEENS CAN GIVE MOTHER DEAR

I happen to be of that generation where we referred to our mothers as "Mother Dear." My mother has gone to her eternal home with God, but I still remember how I always endeavored to show my love to her with gifts at Mother's Day, her birthday, Thanksgiving, Easter and Christmas. I recall how I often did not have much money during my growing-up years. But whatever I gave her, it would make her smile. You see, mothers work hard for us.

Having reached the point where I am now a grandfather, I can now draw on my years of experience and offer this bit of advice, whether you are a teen or otherwise, on how to make your mother smile. I am suggesting gifts that don't require any wrapping paper, or a pretty bag. Why not try them.

⊞ Thank her for the next thing she does for you, whether it's buying your favorite snack or dropping you off at ball practice. "She already know!" you think? Maybe, but everyone enjoys being thanked again.

⊞ Do something she tells you to do without moaning, groaning, or asking, "Do I have to? Right now?" Come on now, be honest. Don't you just automatically question her when she wants dishes done or the trash taken out? It might shock her, but a simple "Yes, Mom," or "Sure," or "Okay," from you would brighten her day considerably.

⊞ Ask her to tell you something she enjoyed when she was your age. People love to talk about themselves, and you might even learn something, especially because most of your conversations with her probably center on you. By doing this, you also show your interest in her as an individual, not just someone put on earth to meet your needs.

▣ Tell her something you like about her, whether it's that she always attends your band concerts, keeps clean clothes in your closet, or listens when you're down. Or maybe you think her eyes are pretty or her singing is beautiful. Whatever it is, let her know in a sincere tone of voice so she understands you mean it. Most moms get very few compliments.

▣ Volunteer to do a chore that she usually does. Maybe you hate cleaning bathrooms, but did you ever think that she may dislike it just as much as you do? And if you don't know how to do it, it's time you learned! I bet you that she will be only too happy to show, it meant that she would not have to do it for a while.

▣ Tell her you'll be praying for her. Don't come across as patronizing. But a sincere offer will usually be accepted. Coming across as her spiritual superior won't be appreciated. You can also find out if she has anything specific she'd like you to bring to God in prayer.

▣ Ask her for advice. If your mother is like most parents, she already gives you lots of ideas about what to do and not to do. But there's something different about having a person really question you about what you think. Choose an area in which you haven't already had an argument and honestly consider what she says. You might actually end up getting some good counsel and wise advice!

It doesn't have to be something critically important like who you should marry, and don't pick a subject you feel super strongly about. But even finding out if she likes a pair of earrings with a certain dress and changing them if she doesn't can help her feel needed and valued by you. That is a precious gift.

⊞ Make an extra effort speak kindly to her. Many teens are so used to talking in a disrespectful way to their parents that they don't even realize they're doing it. Usually it's not the words that are said; it's the tone of voice used. Listen to how you talk to her. Is it sarcastic? Is it superior sounding? Would you speak that way to your friends? Work at trying to change it to sound as if you love her as much as you do.

⊞ Stop expecting her to be perfect. Most little kids think their moms never can be wrong, but as they grow, they should come to see Mom isn't God in miniature. No one is ever going to measure up to Him. If you're still getting upset when she blows it, it's time to face reality. Sure, it may be hard for her to admit it to you, but she makes mistakes many times. What should be your response? Forgive her, just like you'd forgive anyone else who hurts you.

Even if you have already bought your Mom a plant, book, or her favorite fragrance, consider one of the above as an additional present. Your mother will be thrilled! She may even like it so much that you can give it to her again on her birthday. Then there's Valentine's Day, Easter, and Christmas.

Dr. Wright L. Lassiter, Jr.

HOW TO BE A "COOL" DAD

More is taught when a father spends time with his son. By a father's example, a boy navigates toward becoming a man.

In a previous essay I addressed the subject of motherhood and tried to share some of the joys of motherhood based on the life of my mother, and how I was caused to aid her as a "surrogate mother" to my brothers and sisters. Now my focus turns to the father.

It's obvious that for many dads, being buds with their kids is as simple as doing all they can to extend their adolescence. After all, don't most men feel like they're just big kids wrapped in a body that refuses to defy gravity? Having a child somehow gives some men permission to act their shoe size, not their age.

We have all seen those men at the mall, or at the Little League baseball game. When his kid hits a homer, he's the first one off the sidelines to give him a double high-five. Unfortunately, we have also seen some boys in adult bodies take it to extreme and exhibit detestable behavior in their exuberance.

Is this what your child wants? More important is this what your child needs? I have learned, in my mature years, to appreciate the contemporary language of kids. I have learned that "cool" has no relation to the temperature, but it really means that something is good when it is "cool."

In my efforts to understand what "cool" means; I am abstracting here six "cool" things that appeared in an article in the magazine New Man. While it is a decade old, it is still relevant.

Understand your child's embarrassment. Boys don't like hugs in public, even from their dad. Avoid being on a "hug mission" in public. It sometimes hurts, but save the overt affection actions for when you home.

Listen first. I am both a father and a preacher. Every dad has a sermon ready to preach when his kid steps out of line. The "right and wrong" stuff is easy to dish out. And there are times when we need to dish it out. But as the old saying goes, "Timing is everything."

In this article that I am abstracting from, there is the story about the junior high boy who came home one semester with a "D" on a report card otherwise filled with As and Bs. The father's first inclination was to revoke his privileges, make his son quit basketball and cut his allowance in half. When they sat down for "conference," the son was ready for the worst.

The father began by asking his son, "tell me about that D" in a calm tone. "I want to hear your side." After a few stammers, the son talked about the teacher not liking athletes, his desire to do well in more important classes, how everyone hated that teacher . . . and the fact that he had chosen to goof around a bit more than usual.

The father asked, "What do you think I can do to encourage you to take each of your classes a bit more seriously?"

Stunned by his father's low-key blow, the son searched for words. "Well, I guess you could get me talking a little more about each of my classes and remind me to work hard in them all."

The father's response was "that's fair, I can do that. Now what should we do about this D?"

The son said, "Well two weeks without watching sports on TV would probably get my attention."

The "cool dad" fought the urge to grin. The issue was settled and he didn't have to moralize once. All he did was ask questions—and listen.

Use his weaknesses as strength. As a "cool dad," let your kids make fun of you once in a while. When they do that they're making the effort to bring you down to their level. You need to demonstrate to your kid that you are a normal guy with weaknesses. You can be trusted and listened to.

Philippians 2:5-9 illustrates what Jesus did to show us what God was like. He left heaven and became one of us. He laid aside his kingly robes and took the form of a man, became a servant and even died on a cross. His weakness became our strength.

When your son or daughter hits the teen years, they'll need less sermons and more self-revelation. "Failure" stories have the potential to teach more than adult "victorious living" stories. You don't have to tell them all of your deep, dark secrets—just some of them. If they see you as a fallible human—like them—they'll be more likely to talk to you when they blow it. This is what you want anyway.

A "cool dad" isn't embarrassed about his relationship with God. When I carry my Bible with me to places other than church, that act is seen and, I am pleased to say, emulated by others.

The "cool dad" admits his mistakes. In this article there is the incident where the son confronts his dad and says to him, "Ooooh, Dad, you looked at that lady in the tight dress, I saw you." The father responded thusly: "Son, your dad is married. He doesn't need to look at women in skimpy, low-cut dresses."

The story continued with the father saying (to himself) whenever I start talking about myself in the third person, I'm trying to avoid something. Fortunately, for the father, his son did not press the issue. But the father thought that he should have replied thusly: "You're right, son, I did look at her. Men have a tough time not looking at women just for their bodies, even old married guys like your dad. But it's not right, is it? God didn't create women just to be looked at, did He?"

This portion of the article concludes with two words—next time.

The "cool dad" acts like an adult, but understands what it's like to be a kid. They're boys! And dad (like me and other dads) has been given an awesome task in assisting their safe navigation toward becoming men. Sometimes that means remembering the days when life was simple: childhood.

As much as I would like to return to those carefree days, such is not possible. When my son and daughter were growing up, I did live a little through my kids' lives, but I was selective. In my first presidential experience in Upstate New York, my son and I became something of early celebrities. We both appeared in newspaper articles with some regularity. He for his athletic and academic prowess, and me for my exploits as an African American college president. But I kept my part in perspective and let the "kid" always shine.

My son needed me to stay an adult. I was his visible lighthouse, pointing out the rocks and guiding him (and my daughter) to safe harbors. If I acted like a flashlight in the fog, the consequences could have been disastrous.

It's often easy to be a flashlight. But I have always taken the challenge to be an immovable lighthouse. It's what my children need. It's what your children need. It's what they want.[4]

Dr. Wright L. Lassiter, Jr.

---

4   That's what it means to be a "cool dad."

THE GRAND PARENTING YEARS

As the years of marriage pass by and the anniversaries become silver, and hopefully golden, the relationship between wife and husband needs special nourishment. My wife and I have enjoyed forty-nine years of marriage and can speculate on a golden anniversary "just around the corner." My wife has been retired from the nursing profession for over a decade, and I am still as active as ever with my retirement projected to occur at the time of our golden wedding anniversary. Our two children are both past forty, well established in their careers, and each has a daughter. Our daughter and her family live five minutes away. Our son and his family lived seventeen minutes away before he went west to take on the challenge of being a hospital CEO. Empty, but not so empty for there is still close contact.

Our children have had the privilege of spending significant time with my father and mother when they were alive. Therefore they were exposed to the grandparent cycle and pattern at very early ages.

My wife and I were also exposed to grand parenting by observing my parents. We came to realize that grand parenting can become a wonderful gift. Now that we are active grandparents, we are practicing what we observed from my parents. We had learned that we could help our children provide the stability and guidelines that their children needed, in our role as grandparents.

Because you can always "send the grandchild home," we invite them into our home as often as they wish to come. Usually these are only overnight events, but they are important to both grandparent and grandchild. Each gets to know the other while eating a meal, playing a game, watching television together, reading a book together, or just chatting. Such occasions comfortably bridge the generation gap.

We have learned we must not do all the talking; we need to listen without judging. We wanted to get to know those little girls—what they think, what motivates them, what troubles them, what excites them.

We also learned that we have the responsibility of sharing. We can tell what we have learned and felt and experienced. Eric Sevareid says older people help youngsters, who haven't read much history or lived very long reach back into the past. We can help them reach out, because we have experienced so much more through our reading and travel. We can help them learn about their cultural, religious and family heritage. We can help them experience the joy of making gifts for others. We can witness to our faith.

All of this can be done quietly, without fanfare, without intimidation, within an environment that only grandparents may be able to provide in today's fractured and frenetic society.

Gift-giving to grandchildren can become creative. I have found that we can always give a good book, introduce the grandchild to a new hobby, or share a contemporary recording that sings about the Good News rather than despair.

We can also give gifts that last a lifetime. Happy is the grandparent who can share adventures with a grandchild, walking a nature trail, going together to the Science Place (as we often do with our grandchildren), or exploring a museum, or quietly sitting together in church. As a minister, it was my privilege to christen both of my granddaughters, and to also baptize them. They talk about what "papa" did in his robes, and in the water.

If grandchildren live far away, then grandparents will have to plan for visits. They can go themselves, or they can arrange for the youngsters to visit them. My son's wife lives in Houston and I have been impressed with the visits that are made to both Houston and Dallas. The other side of the grand parenting equation also arrange for the granddaughter to come to Houston for a month each summer to participate in a special education program at Texas Southern University.

While this little treatise has focused on the role of my wife and me in grand parenting, I would be remiss if I did not address surrogate grand parenting. There are dozens of children around us (you) who might thrive if we, as grandparents, helped fill their void.

Reaching out is the perfect antidote for loneliness and can help a husband and wife recapture a sense of meaning and purpose for their lives. Reaching out to one's grandchildren and great-grandchildren can renew us, and them.

Finally, we play with our grandchildren and we pray for them. With the psalmist we also petition: "So even to old age and gray hairs, O God, do not forsake (us) till (we) proclaim Thy might to all the generations to come" (Psalm 71:18).

Note: For a much longer treatment of the subject please examine Husbands and Wives: A Guide to Solving Problems and Building Relationships, published by Victor Books.

Dr. Wright L. Lassiter, Jr.

FOREWORD

Read to your children,
Keep your promises
Go for walks together,
Let your children help with household projects,
Spend time one-on-one with each child,
Tell your children about your childhood,
Go to the zoo, movies, museums, ball games as a family,
Set a good example,
Use good manners.

Help your children with homework,
Show your children lots of warmth and affection,
Set clear, consistent limits,
Consider how your decisions will affect your children,
Listen to your children,
Know your children's friends,
Take your children to work with you occasionally.

Open a savings account for college education,
Resolve conflicts quickly,
Take your children to your place of worship,
Make a kite together,
Fly a kite together,
Let your children help you with your chores,
Teach your children how to work.

Do you get the idea? Then work on it!

It takes a man to be a dad!

THE X FILES AND THE TRUTH

On September 10, 1993 a strange new life force was born. "The X Files" burst onto television screens across the United States. Within a few weeks it had attracted unexpectedly large audiences and by the end of the first series had achieved cult status.

Viewers tuned into its unique blend of sleuthing and science fiction. As a result, the program's devotees—known as X-Philes—became experts in extraterrestrials and the paranormal.

Each episode followed FBI agents Fox Mulder (David Duchovny) and Dana Scully (Gillian Anderson) as they attempt to uncover the truth behind some strange and disturbing event.

The title for the series came from the fact that there were a number of cases in the FBI's files that were unexplained—the X files. In the fictional series the U.S. government wants them covered up. Agents Mulder and Scully want to bring them out into the open.

Mulder, the FBI's top crime investigator, is driven by the conviction that there is alien activity in the world.

Scully, a medical doctor, was selected by the FBI as Mulder's partner because of her expertise in forensic medicine and pathology, and to provide rational scientific explanations of the events under investigation.

The series subtitle is "The Truth is Out There." The search for this truth leads the intrepid agents into ever-more-amazing situations. The series seldom provides clear-cut resolutions to the episodes. Loose ends are left dangling, adding to the sense of creepiness the opening music introduces. The truth may be out there, but we seldom find out what it is.

The search for truth is not limited to agents Mulder and Scully. People have always tried to discover the truth behind human existence. It leads them to different directions, sometimes toward a satisfactory answer and sometimes toward danger and destruction.

Yet there is an answer for us all. In John's Gospel Jesus says: "I am the way and the truth and the life" (John 14:6).

If we want to find the true way the answer is simple: follow Jesus. If we want the truth: look at Jesus. To discover real life: believe in Jesus.

Mulder and Scully's fictitious searches lead them into disturbing encounters with frightening creatures. Our legitimate search for truth can lead toward a loving and caring God in whom we find peace of mind and fulfillment, not fear.

BEAUTIFUL YOUTH

It's the face of Youth I behold each day
That makes the day seem bright.
"Have I led Youth safely along the way?"
I will ask myself at night.
Shall I look for beauty or faces fair?
No, rather I'll look for truth;
And if truth is found, then beauty is there,
In the beautiful face of Youth.

It's the hope of the world that listens to me.
God grant that my words ring true,
That they are to Youth what I'd have them be,
And that when the day is through
May the sense of duty fittingly done
Be present my spirit to soothe.
Than a tribute high I'll know I've won
In the beautiful eyes of Youth.

Oh, why should I care for creed or race
Or birth, in a land of the free?
Let me look in the eyes of a youthful face
And read there the pedigree.
Let me learn, through those windows of the soul,
And always remember, immortal and whole
Is the beautiful soul of Youth.

For when all is said and done in the world
And the ends of all things come;
When the banner of God, at last unfurled,

An Outstretched Hand

Calls all of His children home;
If there's one thing endures to the end of all
And proves to be ultimate truth,
I know it now, and it's what I call
The beautiful faith of Youth.

Louis Burton Woodward
State Normal School—Gorham, Maine

"A PARENT'S PRAYER"

"Oh heavenly Father, make me a better parent. Help me to understand my children, to listen patiently to what they have to say and to understand all their questions kindly. Keep me from interrupting them, talking back to them and contradicting them. Make me as courteous to them as I would have them be to me. Give me the courage to confess my sins against my children and ask their forgiveness when I know that I have done wrong.

May I not vainly hurt the feelings of my children. Forbid that I should laugh at their mistakes, or resort to shame and ridicule as punishment. Let me not tempt a child to lie or steal. So guide me hour by hour that I may demonstrate by all I say and do that honesty produces happiness.

Reduce, I pray, the meanness in me. May I cease to nag; and I am out of sorts; help me, Oh Lord, to hold my tongue. Blind me to the little errors of my children and help me to see the good things they do. Give me a ready word for honest praise.

Help me to treat my children as those of their own age, but let me not exact of them the judgments and conventions of adults. Allow me not to rob them of the opportunity to wait upon themselves, to think, to choose, and to make their own decisions.

Forbid that I should ever punish them for my selfish satisfaction. May I grant them all their wishes that are reasonable and have the courage always to withhold a privilege that I know will do them harm.

Make me so fair and just, so considerate and companionable to my children that they will have genuine esteem for me. Fit me to be loved and imitated by my children. Oh God, do give me calm and poise and self-control."

Prayer by Garry C. Myers
Founder of <u>Highlights for Children</u> Magazine

HOW TO TEACH A CHILD . . . .

I tried to teach my child
with books.
He only gave me
puzzled looks.

I tried to teach my child with words,
They passed him by,
Oft unheard.

Despairingly, I turned aside;
"How shall I teach this child,"
I cried.

"Come," said he,
"Play with me."

"Teachers do it for the outcome, not the income."

(Author Unknown)

THE MAN WHO PLAYS
THE GAME . . .

"The credit in life does not go the critic who stands on the sideline and points out where the strong stumble, but rather the real credit in life goes to the man who is actually in the arena, whose face may get marred by sweat and dust, who knows great enthusiasm and great devotion and learns to spend himself in a worthy cause, who, at best if he wins, knows the thrill of great achievement and if he fails, at least fails while daring greatly, so that in life his place will never be with those very cold and timid souls who know neither factory nor defeat."

— Theodore Roosevelt

I SHALL USE MY TIME

"I would rather be ashes than dust.
I would rather my spark should burn out
in a brilliant blaze.

Than it should be stifled in dry-rot …
Man's chief purpose is to LIVE, not exist.
I shall not waste my days trying
to prolong them.
I shall USE my TIME!"

— Jack London

SUCCESS...

To laugh often and much;
to win the respect of intelligent people;
to earn the appreciation of honest critics;
and endure the betrayal of false friends.

To appreciate beauty;
to leave the world a bit better;
whether by a healthy child,
a garden patch or a
redeemed social condition;

To know even one life has breather easier,
because you have lived, this is to have succeeded.

— Ralph Waldo Emerson

PART V

END NOTES

ABOUT THE AUTHOR

Dr. Wright L. Lassiter, Jr.

Wright L. Lassiter, Jr. was named Chancellor of the seven-college Dallas County Community College District in May 2006. Prior to that, he served for twenty years as the President of El Centro College of the Dallas County Community College District.

Dr. Lassiter previously served as President of Bishop College in Dallas; President of Schenectady County Community College in New York; Vice President of Finance and Management at Morgan State University in Baltimore, and Business Manager of Tuskegee University in Alabama.

He is Chairman of the Board of Trustees of the African American Museum, Past Board Chairman and Senior Director of the Urban League of Greater Dallas and North Texas, Inc., trustee of Dallas Baptist University and Parker College of Chiropractic in Dallas; and serves on several other boards that include the North Texas Commission, the YMCA Foundation, the Dallas Baptist University Foundation, the University of Texas Southwestern Medical School Foundation, and the Dallas Citizens Council.

He has held two presidential appointment: the White House Commission on Minority Business Development and the National Advisory Council to the National Endowment for the Humanities. Both presidential appointments required confirmation by the Senate of the United States. At the state level his appointments included six-year terms on the boards of the Texas Guaranteed Student Loan Corporation and the Texas Council on the Humanities. He also served a six-year term on the Board of Advisors of the Hankamer School of Business at Baylor University.

He is a Distinguished Adjunct Professor of Management, Ethics & Leadership at Dallas Baptist University and holds an honorary Doctor of Humanities degree from that institution.

He holds a B.S. degree, magna cum laude, from Alcorn State University, an MBA degree (with high honors) from Indiana University-Bloomington, and an Ed.D. degree from Auburn University. He has pursued further advanced studies at Princeton University and Oxford University. In 1995, the Kelley School of Business at Indiana University-Bloomington elected Dr. Lassiter to the Indiana University Academy of Alumni Fellows. In 2007 he was elected to the National Advisory Council to the Graduate School of Education at Auburn University.

He is the recipient of numerous honors and awards at the state, regional and national levels. He was a member of the inaugural class of inductees into the African American Educators Hall of Fame in Dallas.

Among his published works are four books published by Trafford Publishing Group: <u>Make an IMPACT, not just an IMPRESSION</u>, <u>The Words of a College President</u>, <u>The Ask-back Letters,</u> and <u>The Power of Prayer.</u>

He is married to Bessie R. Lassiter and they have two adult children: Michele Lassiter-Ewell (Cylton) of Dallas, TX and their son (co-author) Wright L. Lassiter, III (Cathy) of Castro Valley, CA; and two grandchildren, Ryan and Loren.

ABOUT THE AUTHOR

Wright L. Lassiter, III

Wright L. Lassiter, III was named Chief Executive Officer of Alameda County Medical Center in September 2005. Alameda County Medical Center is a comprehensive health system comprised of three hospitals, and three community-based clinics. Located east of San Francisco, Ca, the safety-net health system serves the residents of Oakland, Berkeley, and the greater metropolitan areas of Alameda County.

Mr. Lassiter previously held the position of Senior Vice President, Operations for JPS Health Network, an integrated health system serving the residents of Fort Worth and Arlington, Texas and the greater metropolitan area of Tarrant County. Lassiter began his career in healthcare administration at Methodist Health System (Dallas, Texas) in 1990. He served in various capacities during his decade-long tenure at Methodist, culminating as Vice President for Methodist-Dallas Medical Center.

Lassiter currently holds a number of community and corporate board appointments in Northern California. He serves on the Board of Directors for the Beta Healthcare Group, the Oakland Metropolitan Chamber of Commerce, the Alameda Alliance for Health, the YMCA of the East Bay, and the Bay Area Urban Network. Additionally, he serves on the Safety Net Advisory Board of the California Regional Health Information Organization (Cal-RHIO).

On a state and national level, Lassiter currently serves as President-Elect of the Board of Directors for the California Association of Public Hospitals and Health Systems. He also serves on the Board of Directors for the Safety Net Institute, and the National Association of Public Hospitals.

In previous communities, Lassiter has served on the Boards of the Salvation Army of Metropolitan Dallas, the YMCA of Dallas, Citizens Development Center, the YMCA of Fort Worth, and the Fort Worth Metropolitan Black Chamber of Commerce. He also served as a mentor in the Minority Achievers Program, and served on the Advisory Board for the Project Tomorrow.

He holds a Bachelors Degree (with honors) in Chemistry from LeMoyne College (Syracuse, NY) and a Masters in Healthcare Administration Degree (valedictorian) from Indiana University (Indianapolis, IN).

He is the recipient of numerous awards including: Bay Area Excellence in Public Service, a Minority Achiever Award, and the Urban Health Care Award.

He is married to Cathy J. Lassiter. They are the proud parents of an 11-year old daughter (Loren) and reside in Castro Valley, California.